ORWELL ON TRUTH

BOOKS BY GEORGE ORWELL

Down and Out in Paris and London

Burmese Days

A Clergyman's Daughter

Keep the Aspidistra Flying

The Road to Wigan Pier

Homage to Catalonia

Coming Up for Air

Inside the Whale and Other Essays

The Lion and the Unicorn

Animal Farm

Critical Essays (American title, *Dickens, Dali & Others*)

Nineteen Eighty-Four

Shooting an Elephant and Other Essays

Such, Such Were the Joys

The Complete Works of George Orwell (20 vols.)

Orwell in Spain

The Orwell Reader: Fiction, Essays, and Reportage

The Collected Essays, Journalism, and Letters of George Orwell (4 vols.)

A Collection of Essays

Nineteen Eighty-Four: The Facsimile

GEORGE ORWELL

ORWELL ON TRUTH

Mariner Books
Houghton Mifflin Harcourt
Boston   New York

First Mariner Books edition 2019
Copyright © 2017 by the Estate of the late Sonia Brownell Orwell
Compilation copyright © 2017 by Harvill Secker
Introduction copyright © 2018 by Adam Hochschild
First published in Great Britain in 2017 by Harvill Secker

For information about permission to reproduce selections from this
book, write to trade.permissions@hmhco.com or to Permissions,
Houghton Mifflin Harcourt Publishing Company,
3 Park Avenue, 19th Floor, New York, New York 10016.

hmhbooks.com

This volume, compiled by David Milner, was collected from
The Complete Works of George Orwell, edited by Peter Davison, OBE,
published in Great Britain in 1998 by Secker & Warburg.

Library of Congress Cataloging-in-Publication Data
Names: Orwell, George, 1903–1950 author. |
Hochschild, Adam author of introduction.
Title: Orwell on truth / George Orwell.
Description: Boston : Houghton Mifflin Harcourt, 2018.
Identifiers: LCCN 2017057698 | ISBN 9781328507860 (hardback) |
978-1-328-50871-3 (ebook) | ISBN 978-0-358-06505-0 (pbk.)
Subjects: LCSH: Orwell, George, 1903–1950—
Political and social views. | Truthfulness and falsehood—
Political aspects. | BISAC: LITERARY COLLECTIONS / Essays. |
POLITICAL SCIENCE / Public Policy / Social Policy.
| POLITICAL SCIENCE / Political Freedom & Security / General.
Classification: LCC PR6029.R8 A6 2018 | DDC 828/.91209—dc23
LC record available at https://lccn.loc.gov/2017057698

Printed in the United States of America
DOC 10 9 8 7 6 5 4 3 2 1

INTRODUCTION

IN THINKING ABOUT a long-dead writer, we sometimes wonder: what would he or she make of the world today? Even though he died nearly 70 years ago, George Orwell often seems as if he *were* writing about the world today.

Could we have a better guide to Donald Trump's America? When a senior aide to President Trump talked about "alternative facts" at a time when the real ones (a low turnout for his inauguration, starkly visible in photographs) were embarrassing, what is that but the twisting of truth into propaganda that Orwell described so chillingly in *Nineteen Eighty-Four* and elsewhere? In a 1943 essay excerpted in this book he wrote, "Nazi theory . . . specifically denies that such a thing as 'the truth' exists . . . If the Leader says of such and such an event, 'It never happened'—well, it never happened. If he says that two and two are five—well, two and two are five. This prospect frightens me much more than bombs." Is this not the universe that President Trump, surrounded by embarrassing facts on all sides, would like to live in?

Similarly, when Trump speaks of Mexican immigrants, saying, "They're bringing drugs. They're bringing crime. They're rapists," this is a mindset Orwell knew well, for he writes in another piece in these pages of "the habit of assuming that human beings can be classified like insects and that whole blocks of millions or tens of millions of people can be confidently labelled 'good' or 'bad.'"

Or, take a further Orwell insight that seems based on today's headlines: "All nationalists have the power of not seeing resemblances between similar sets of facts. A British Tory will defend self-determination in Europe and oppose it in India with no feeling of inconsistency. Actions are held to be good or bad, not on their own merits but according to who does them." As I write this, Trump has just addressed the United Nations General Assembly, praising the principle of "sovereignty" and condemning nations like North Korea and Iran that he accuses of threatening the sovereignty of other countries, but not mentioning the outright seizure of Crimea from sovereign Ukraine by the autocrat he so much admires, Vladimir Putin of Russia.

Lest we forget, open contempt for facts is not new. It was an unnamed member of President George W. Bush's staff in 2004 who, interviewed by the *New York Times Magazine*, sneeringly referred to "the reality-based community." He added, "That's not the way the world really works anymore. We're an empire now, and when we act, we create our own reality." Consider just one topic: climate change. For decades, after an immense propaganda effort financed by oil companies, an appalling number of Americans have vociferously denied that human beings have anything to do with climate change. As a succession of unusually severe hurricanes lash our land and rising ocean waters flood our shores, could even Orwell have imagined such a defiant assertion that two and two equal five? All of us in the reality-based community need him more than ever.

• • •

As this collection makes clear, Orwell valued truth above all else. And he detested political lies, sometimes even more than violence. What gave Orwell his uncanny truth-seeking radar? I believe it can be traced to several key experiences. Literate and well read though he was, his was a life lived in the real world, bringing him face-to-face with ruthless forces that on one occasion almost killed him. As the critic Christopher Hitchens once said, Orwell personally encountered the three great malevolent movements of the twentieth century—European imperialism, fascism, and communism—and took the right stand on all three.

Imperialism was the first. He had been born in India, where his father was a colonial civil servant. Although Orwell was taken back to England as a small child, he had long dreamed of returning to the East. After finishing his schooling, he set off in 1922, at the age of nineteen, to join the Indian Imperial Police in Burma, which was then governed as part of British India. Learning to speak the local language, he found the British Empire to be a far more brutal and less glorious enterprise than what he had imagined. After five years — "I had already made up my mind that imperialism was an evil thing and the sooner I chucked up my job and got out of it the better" — he returned to England, determined to become a writer.

Many intellectuals of the day criticized imperialism from the safety of their desks, but it was rare indeed for such an opponent to emerge from the colonial bureaucracy itself, especially from the police. Surely Orwell's feelings were heightened by the conflict between his beliefs and the role that he had found himself in. He explored those emotions in his novel *Burmese Days,* excerpted here, and in two essays, "A Hanging" and "Shooting an Elephant."

The latter is a particularly brilliant piece of writing, in which Orwell describes how, as a police officer, he was confronted with an elephant that had broken free of its chain and killed someone. Once he saw the situation, he realized that elephant didn't have to be killed in return, only guarded carefully until its mahout, whom it would obey, arrived on the scene. But a crowd of angry Burmese was demanding that he shoot the elephant, and he knew he would lose face if he did not. "A sahib has got to act like a sahib; he has got to appear resolute." For every such official "it is the condition of his rule that he shall spend his life in trying to impress the 'natives' and so in every crisis he has got to do what the 'natives' expect of him . . . My whole life, every white man's life in the East, was one long struggle not to be laughed at." He shot the elephant. I once assigned this essay in a narrative writing workshop I was teaching in India, not at all sure of how Indian students would react to a former colonial officer baring the conflict in his soul. But they were deeply impressed. One, speaking of Orwell's painstaking honesty about his own conflicted feelings, said, "I didn't know it was possible to write like that."

Soon after a disillusioned Orwell returned to Europe from seeing imperialism firsthand in Burma, like millions of others he became deeply alarmed by the rise of another powerful system: fascism. Benito Mussolini had been in office in

Italy since the early 1920s, and then Adolf Hitler took power in Germany in 1933. Suddenly Western Europe's largest and most powerful country was under a dictator's rule. That dictator was issuing laws restricting Jews, sending soldiers goose-stepping through the streets, and ordering his party's thugs to beat and murder his political enemies. Ominously, half a dozen other European countries, from Portugal to Lithuania, Hungary to Greece, were also under regimes of the far right. In England itself, the British Union of Fascists boasted 50,000 members; wearing black tunics, black trousers, and wide black leather belts, they paraded through Jewish neighborhoods of London under a flag with a lightning bolt, shouting insults, giving the straight-arm salute, and beating up anyone in their way. As the French writer André Malraux put it, "Fascism has spread its great black wings over Europe."

In 1936, the brewing tension between fascism and democracy abruptly broke into outright war. In Spain, a large group of far-right army officers staged a military coup against the elected government of the Spanish Republic. In the first weeks of fighting, the plotters seized roughly a third of Spain. Germany and Italy rushed aid to the Nationalists, as the rebellious right-wing officers called themselves: military advisers, artillery, ammunition, the latest tanks, and fighter aircraft and crews to fly them. Mussolini would before long send some 80,000 ground troops as well. It was instantly clear that if the Nationalists won the Spanish Civil War, Hitler and Mussolini would have a new ally. The beleaguered Spanish Republic appealed desperately for aid, and soon volunteers from more than 50 countries came to Spain to fight in its defense. One of them was George Orwell. He arrived in Barcelona just after Christmas of 1936 and immediately joined a militia unit at the front. His memoir of the next six months, *Homage to Catalonia,* is his greatest work of nonfiction.

But it was not only fascism that Orwell came up against in Spain. There was something of a civil war within the civil war, for politics on the Republican side of the front lines was bewilderingly complex. Britain, France, and the United States, not wanting to get drawn into a new European war, had all refused to sell arms to the Spanish Republic. Eventually the only major country that did so was not another democracy but Joseph Stalin's Soviet Union. And Stalin demanded political favors in return: high positions for both Spanish and Soviet Communists in the Republic's government, armed forces, and police.

The ruthless and paranoid Stalin had no tolerance for any kind of dissent within the world Communist movement. At home, anyone who questioned his authority was shot or sent to the *gulag*. Prominent renegades abroad, like his archenemy Leon Trotsky, often ended up assassinated. In Spain, where the Republic's coalition government was highly fractious, Stalin repeatedly pushed it to suppress a small left-wing party that was critical of the Soviet Union. Orwell, as it happened, had joined the militia unit of that party, the Partido Obrero de Unificación Marxista, or POUM. At one point, coming to Barcelona from the front for what he had hoped would be a week's leave, he became caught up in bloody street fighting between the POUM and its political allies on one side and the Communist-dominated police on the other. That fighting ended in a truce, and a shaken Orwell returned to the war.

A few weeks later, he narrowly escaped death. He was supervising a change of sentries in his frontline trench when a Nationalist bullet passed through his neck, just missing his carotid artery. After a spell in military hospitals Orwell received permission to leave the army and again returned to Barcelona. There, he planned to meet his wife, who had been working at a POUM English-language newspaper, and go back to England. To his dismay, when he reached the city, he had to go underground: the POUM and its publications had been banned and many of its leaders and supporters thrown in jail. Several of them, including a Scottish fellow soldier whom Orwell knew well, would die there. After he spent several nights in hiding, one of them sleeping in a vacant lot, he and his wife were finally able to slip out of the country a few days later.

For him, the most searing part of this experience was seeing the lies that surrounded it. Whatever the deficiencies of the POUM—and even Orwell felt it suffered from "revolutionary purism"—he and his fellow militiamen had spent months in cold, muddy trenches, risking their lives in the fight against fascism. But Communists had thoroughly taken control of the Spanish Republic's propaganda machinery and claimed the POUM was in league with the Nationalists, sending them military secrets in invisible ink and in clandestine radio transmissions. Foreign reporters tended to repeat what the Republic's spokespeople told them, and even the *New York Times* and Ernest Hemingway, in Spain reporting for a US newspaper syndicate, published some of these canards. Soon afterward, the London *Daily Worker,* the British Communist newspaper, charged that

Orwell himself had periodically left the POUM trenches to make secret rendezvous with Nationalist troops in no-man's-land.

Seeing himself and his fellow antifascists the objects of such preposterous charges had an immense impact on Orwell, and would be reflected, more than a decade later in *Nineteen Eighty-Four,* in his excoriating portrait of the Ministry of Truth. Just as he had sensed the hypocrisy at the heart of British imperialism and the malice in Hitler's scapegoating of the Jews, here was yet a third totalitarian system that depended on the power of the lie. Small wonder that, having lived through all of this before he even turned thirty-five, Orwell was to become his century's greatest truth teller.

This collection, drawn from his books, essays, letters, and to a large extent from his journalism, shows Orwell's truth-seeking radar at work in every direction. From the British Empire, to contemporary writers, to the media, to Joseph Stalin, to nationalism ("not to be confused with patriotism"), from the politics of the

English language to the publication of *Animal Farm,* Orwell mercilessly attacks propaganda and dishonesty everywhere he sees it. As he puts it in one essay, "The first thing that we ask of a writer is that he shan't tell lies." It was his credo.

So what would he make of our sorry world today? It's not hard to guess, since he predicted so many dimensions of it. Even though he lived in the infancy of television and of electronic surveillance, for example, he nonetheless foresaw their power, and, in *Nineteen Eighty-Four,* combined them into one instrument, the telescreen. In homes and offices throughout the fictional superpower in his novel, telescreens both ceaselessly broadcast propaganda and monitor everyone's behavior. Would he be surprised at Edward Snowden's revelations of the pervasive way in which the US government eavesdrops on millions of people's emails and cell phones, at home and abroad? Or would he be surprised that we've ended up with a reality-TV star as president? Orwell seems to have seen it all coming.

Welcome, then, to this array of excerpts from his writing. Think of them not as a main dish, but as a tasting menu. For the full power of his eloquence, you have to read his works whole, whether they be novels like *Nineteen Eighty-Four,* which evokes an entire dystopian world, or a memoir like *Down and Out in Paris and London,* or the letters in which he is as forceful and clear-sighted writing to a friend as to a wider audience, or the great essay about his school days, "Such, Such Were the Joys . . . ," which shows that there can be hypocrisy and abuse of power in a provincial boarding school just as there is in a police state. But this is an excellent place to start, or to sample the full range of Orwell's targets for readers who know him only from *Nineteen Eighty-Four* or *Animal Farm.* Throughout all he wrote, he evinces the hope that by speaking honestly about the world as he saw it, he could help others, as well, to see through its pretenses, falsehoods, and illusions. In hard times, that's a worthy faith.

ADAM HOCHSCHILD

ORWELL ON TRUTH

'The truth about the English and their Empire'

from *Burmese Days* (1934)

[FLORY] CELEBRATED his twenty-seventh birthday in hospital, covered from head to foot with hideous sores which were called mud-sores, but were probably caused by whisky and bad food. They left little pits in his skin which did not disappear for two years. Quite suddenly he had begun to look and feel very much older. His youth was finished. Eight years of Eastern life, fever, loneliness and intermittent drinking, had set their mark on him.

Since then, each year had been lonelier and more bitter than the last. What was at the centre of all his thoughts now, and what poisoned everything, was the ever bitterer hatred of the atmosphere of imperialism in which he lived. For as his brain developed – you cannot stop your brain developing, and it is one of the tragedies of the half-educated that they develop late, when they are already committed to some wrong way of life – he had grasped the truth about the English and their Empire. The Indian Empire is a despotism – benevolent, no doubt, but still a despotism with theft as its final object. And as to the English of the East, the *sahiblog*, Flory had come so to hate them from living in their society, that he was quite incapable of being fair to them. For after all, the poor devils are no worse than anybody else. They lead unenviable lives; it is a poor bargain to spend thirty years, ill-paid, in an alien country, and then come home with a wrecked liver and a pineapple backside from sitting in cane chairs, to settle down as the bore of some second-rate Club. On the other hand, the *sahiblog* are not to be idealised. There is a prevalent idea that the men at the 'outposts of Empire' are at least able and hardworking. It is a delusion. Outside the scientific services – the Forest Department, the Public Works Department and the like – there is no particular need for a British official in India to do his job competently. Few of them work as hard or as intelligently as the postmaster of a provincial town in England. The real work of administration is done mainly by native subordinates; and the real backbone of the despotism is not the officials but the Army. Given the Army, the officials and the business men can rub along safely enough even if they are fools. And most of them are fools. A dull, decent people, cherishing and fortifying their dullness behind a quarter of a million bayonets.

It is a stifling, stultifying world in which to live. It is a world in which every word and every thought is censored. In England it is hard even to imagine such an atmosphere. Everyone is free in England; we sell our souls in public and buy them back in private, among our friends. But even friendship can hardly exist when every white man is a cog in the wheels of despotism. Free speech is unthinkable. All other kinds of freedom are permitted. You are free to be a drunkard, an idler, a coward, a backbiter, a fornicator; but you are not free to think for yourself. Your opinion on every subject of any conceivable importance is dictated for you by the pukka sahibs' code.

In the end the secrecy of your revolt poisons you like a secret disease. Your whole life is a life of lies. Year after year you sit in Kipling-haunted little Clubs, whisky to right of you, Pink'un to left of you, listening and eagerly agreeing while Colonel Bodger develops his theory that these bloody Nationalists should be boiled in oil. You hear your Oriental friends called 'greasy little *babus*', and you admit, dutifully, that they *are* greasy little *babus*. You see louts fresh from school kicking grey-haired servants. The time comes when you burn with hatred of your own countrymen, when you long for a native rising to drown their Empire in blood. And in this there is nothing honourable, hardly even any sincerity. For, *au fond*, what do you care if the Indian Empire is a despotism, if Indians are bullied and exploited? You only care because the right of free speech is denied you. You are a creature of the despotism, a pukka sahib, tied tighter than a monk or a savage by an unbreakable system of taboos.

YOU ARE FREE TO BE

A DRUNKARD,
AN IDLER,
A COWARD,
A BACKBITER,
A FORNICATOR;

BUT

YOU ARE
NOT FREE TO

TH?NK

FOR YOURSELF.

'In England we tamely admit to being robbed in order to keep half a million worthless idlers in luxury, but we would fight to the last man sooner than be ruled by Chinamen'

from *The Road to Wigan Pier* (1937)

I WAS IN THE Indian Police five years, and by the end of that time I hated the imperialism I was serving with a bitterness which I probably cannot make clear. In the free air of England that kind of thing is not fully intelligible. [. . .] From the most unexpected people, from gin-pickled old scoundrels high up in the Government service, I have heard some such remark as: 'Of course we've no right in this blasted country at all. Only now we're here for God's sake let's stay here.' The truth is that no modern man, in his heart of hearts, believes that it is right to invade a foreign country and hold the population down by force. Foreign oppression is a much more obvious, understandable evil than economic oppression. Thus in England we tamely admit to being robbed in order to keep half a million worthless idlers in luxury, but we would fight to the last man sooner than be ruled by Chinamen; similarly, people who live on unearned dividends without a single qualm of conscience, see clearly enough that it is wrong to go and lord it in a foreign country where you are not wanted. The result is that every Anglo-Indian is haunted by a sense of guilt which he usually conceals as best he can, because there is no freedom of speech, and merely to be overheard making a seditious remark may damage his career. All over India there are Englishmen who secretly loathe the system of which they are part; and just occasionally, when they are quite certain of being in the right company, their hidden bitterness overflows. I remember a night I spent on the train with a man in the Educational Service, a stranger to myself whose name I never discovered. It was too hot to sleep and we spent the night in talking. Half an hour's cautious questioning decided each of us that the other was 'safe'; and then for hours, while the train jolted slowly through the pitch-black night, sitting up in our bunks with bottles of beer handy, we damned the British Empire – damned it from the inside, intelligently and intimately. It did us both good. But we had been speaking forbidden things, and in the haggard morning light when the train crawled into Mandalay, we parted as guiltily as any adulterous couple.

'Let's all get together and have a good hate.'

from *Coming Up for Air* (June 1939)

HILDA SAID SHE WAS going to the Left Book Club meeting. It seemed that there was a chap coming down from London to lecture, though needless to say Hilda didn't know what the lecture was going to be about. I told her I'd go with her. In a general way I'm not much of a one for lectures, but the visions of war I'd had that morning, starting with the bomber flying over the train, had put me into a kind of thoughtful mood. After the usual argument we got the kids to bed early and cleared off in time for the lecture, which was billed for eight o'clock.

It was a misty kind of evening, and the hall was cold and not too well lighted. It's a little wooden hall with a tin roof, the property of some Nonconformist sect or other, and you can hire it for ten bob. The usual crowd of fifteen or sixteen people had rolled up. On the front of the platform there was a yellow placard announcing that the lecture was on 'The Menace of Fascism'. [. . .]

At the beginning I wasn't exactly listening. The lecturer was rather a mean-looking little chap, but a good speaker. White face, very mobile mouth, and the rather grating voice that they get from constant speaking. Of course he was pitching into Hitler and the Nazis. I wasn't particularly keen to hear what he was saying – get the same stuff in the *News Chronicle* every morning – but his voice came across to me as a kind of burr-burr-burr, with now and again a phrase that stuck out and caught my attention.

'Bestial atrocities . . . Hideous outbursts of sadism . . . Rubber truncheons . . . Concentration camps . . . Iniquitous persecution of the Jews . . . Back to the Dark Ages . . . European civilisation . . . Act before it is too late . . . Indignation of all decent peoples . . . Alliance of the democratic nations . . . Firm stand . . . Defence of democracy . . . Democracy . . . Fascism . . . Democracy . . . Fascism . . . Democracy . . .'

You know the line of talk. These chaps can churn it out by the hour. Just like a gramophone.

Turn the handle, press the button and it starts. Democracy, Fascism, Democracy. But somehow it interested me to watch him. A rather mean little man, with a white face and a bald head, standing on a platform, shooting out slogans. What's he doing? Quite deliberately, and quite openly, he's stirring up hatred. Doing his damnedest to make you hate certain foreigners called Fascists. It's a queer thing, I thought, to be known as 'Mr. So-and-so, the well-known anti-Fascist'. A queer trade, anti-Fascism. This fellow, I suppose, makes his living by writing books against Hitler. But what did he do before Hitler came along? And what'll he do if Hitler ever disappears? Same question applies to doctors, detectives, ratcatchers and so forth, of course. But the grating voice went on and on, and another thought struck me. He *means* it. Not faking at all—feels every word he's saying. He's trying to work up hatred in the audience, but that's nothing to the hatred he feels himself. Every slogan's gospel truth to him. [. . .]

I'd stopped listening to the actual words of the lecture. But there are more ways than one of listening. I shut my eyes for a moment. The effect of that was curious. I seemed to see the fellow much better when I could only hear his voice. It was a voice that sounded as if it could go on for a fortnight without stopping. It's a ghastly thing, really, to have a sort of human barrel-organ shooting propaganda at you by the hour. The same thing over and over again. Hate, hate, hate. Let's all get together and have a good hate. Over and over. It gives you the feeling that something has got inside your skull and is hammering down on your brain. But for a moment, with my eyes shut, I managed to turn the tables on him. I got inside *his* skull. It was a peculiar sensation. For about a second I was inside him, you might almost say I *was* him. At any rate, I felt what he was feeling.

I saw the vision that he was seeing. And it wasn't at all the kind of vision that can be talked about. What he's *saying* is merely that Hitler's after us and we must all get together and have a good hate. Doesn't go into details. Leaves it all respectable. But what he's *seeing* is something quite different. It's a picture of himself smashing people's faces in with a spanner. Fascist faces, of course. I *know* that's what he was seeing. It was what I saw myself for the second or two that I was inside him. Smash! Right in the middle! The bones cave in like an eggshell and what was a face a minute ago is just a great big blob of strawberry jam. Smash! There goes another! That's what's in his mind, waking and sleeping, and the more he thinks of it the more he likes it. And it's all OK because the smashed faces belong to Fascists. You could hear all that in the tone of his voice.

But why? Likeliest explanation, because he's scared. Every thinking person nowadays is stiff with fright. This is merely a chap who's got sufficient foresight to be a little more frightened than the others. Hitler's after us! Quick! Let's all grab a spanner and get together, and perhaps if we smash in enough faces they won't smash ours. Gang up, choose your Leader. Hitler's black and Stalin's white. But it might just as well be the other way about, because in the little chap's mind both Hitler and Stalin are the same. Both mean spanners and smashed faces.

War! I started thinking about it again. It's coming soon, that's certain. But who's afraid of war? That's to say, who's afraid of the bombs and the machine-guns? 'You are,' you say. Yes, I am, and so's anybody who's ever seen them. But it isn't the war that matters, it's the after-war. The world we're going down into, the kind of hate-world, slogan-world. The coloured shirts, the barbed wire, the rubber truncheons. The secret cells where the electric light burns night and day, and the detectives watching you while you sleep. And the processions and the posters with enormous faces, and the crowds of a million people all cheering for the Leader till they deafen themselves into thinking that they really worship him, and all the time, underneath, they hate him so that they want to puke. It's all going to happen. Or isn't it? Some days I know it's impossible, other days I know it's inevitable. That night, at any rate, I knew it was going to happen. It was all in the sound of the little lecturer's voice.

'It is good history, if mediocre fiction.'

from review of *World's End* by Upton Sinclair,
Tribune, 13 September 1940

I HAVE NEVER QUITE been able to make up my mind whether Mr. Upton Sinclair is a very good novelist or a very bad one. Since I have continued to read him for many a long year the question might seem to have answered itself, if I could say that I got the same kind of pleasure out of his novels that I got out of others. But in any case, what is a novel? The mere fact that *Tom Jones*, *Sons and Lovers*, *Gentlemen Prefer Blondes*, and *Tarzan of the Apes* are all classed as novels is enough to show one how vague the category is.

Mr. Sinclair's books, also classed as novels, are actually tracts, a sort of Socialist adaptation of the old-style religious tract in which the young man who is on the road to ruin hears a striking sermon and thereafter touches nothing stronger than cocoa. What gave these things the literary power they often possessed was the fact that their authors believed in them; it was certainly not that they showed any knowledge of real life or any sense of character. It is rather the same with Mr. Sinclair. He knows, just as the Hebrew prophets knew, that the world is full of evil, and the depth of his feeling gives life to a series of tremendous sermons that probably lose rather than gain by being cast in story form.

At different times he has written 'show-ups' of the press, the coal trade, the meat trade, the oil trade and I forget what else. This time, in *World's End*, it is the armaments racket. When you know that Lanny Budd, the hero, is a gifted and warm-hearted American boy who has been brought up in the most cultivated European society on the proceeds of his father's thriving trade in machine guns, hand grenades and other instruments of murder, you know the story, more or less. For here, as in all Mr. Sinclair's books, there is not properly speaking any plot, merely the unfolding of a social theme and the story of one individual's growing awareness of it, with conversion to Socialism somewhere about the last chapter.

Where Mr. Sinclair does excel, however, is in his facts. He has probably laid bare more iniquities than any writer of our time, and you can be sure in every case that he is telling you no more than the truth and even a little less than the truth. I have no doubt that the detailed accounts of barefaced swindling and cynical, conscious war-mongering by Sir Basil Zaharoff and others (for real personages come into the book) that are given here are perfectly accurate. No one has ever won a libel action against Mr. Sinclair—which, when you consider the charges he has made, tells one something about present-day society.

Whether his indictments of capitalism have ever made much impression, outside the ranks of the already-converted, is a different question. His best and one of his earliest books, *The Jungle*, a dreadful exposé of labour conditions in the Chicago meat-yards, was truly moving, if only because the fate of poor European peasants lured to America to be worked to death as factory drudges was a pitiful thing in itself. But only one of the book's revelations really got home on the public mind—that conditions in the meat-yards were dirty and infected carcases were often offered for sale. The sufferings of the labourers went unnoticed. 'I had aimed at the public's heart,' Upton Sinclair wrote later, 'and I hit its stomach.' I doubt whether he will hit any part of its anatomy with *World's End*, which deals with a phase of society that has now passed away. But it puts some interesting pieces of blackguardism on record. It is good history, if mediocre fiction.

'It is known that the newspapers are habitually untruthful, but it is also known that they cannot tell lies of more than a certain magnitude'

review of *The Invasion from Mars* by Hadley Cantril, *The New Statesman and Nation,* 26 October 1940

NEARLY TWO YEARS AGO Mr. Orson Welles produced on the Columbia Broadcasting System in New York a radio play based on H. G. Wells's fantasia *The War of the Worlds.* The broadcast was not intended as a hoax, but it had an astonishing and unforeseen result. Thousands mistook it for a news broadcast and actually believed for a few hours that the Martians had invaded America and were marching across the countryside on steel legs a hundred feet high, massacring all and sundry with their heat rays. Some of the listeners were so panic-stricken that they leapt into their cars and fled. Exact figures are, of course, unobtainable, but the compilers of this survey (it was made by one of the research departments of Princeton) have reason to think that about six million people heard the broadcast and that well over a million were in some degree affected by the panic.

At the time this affair caused amusement all over the world, and the credulity of 'those Americans' was much commented on. However, most of the accounts that appeared abroad were somewhat misleading. The text of the Orson Welles production is given in full, and it appears that apart from the opening announcement and a piece of dialogue towards the end the whole play is done in the form of news bulletins, ostensibly real bulletins with names of stations attached to them. This is a natural enough method of producing a play of that type, but it was also natural that many people who happened to turn on the radio after the play had started should imagine that they were listening to a news broadcast. There were therefore two separate acts of belief involved: (i) that the play was a news bulletin, and (ii) that a news bulletin can be taken as truthful. And it is just here that the interest of the investigation lies.

In the U.S.A. the wireless is the principal vehicle of news. There is a great number of broadcasting stations, and virtually every family owns a radio. The authors even make the surprising statement that it is more usual to possess a radio than to take in a newspaper. Therefore, to transfer this incident to England, one has perhaps to imagine the news of the Martian invasion appearing on the front page of one of the evening papers. Undoubtedly such a thing would cause a great stir. It is known that the newspapers are habitually untruthful, but it is also known that they cannot tell lies of more than a certain magnitude and anyone seeing huge headlines in their paper announcing the arrival of a cylinder from Mars would probably believe what he read, at any rate for the few minutes that would be needed to make some verification.

The truly astonishing thing, however, was that so few of the listeners attempted any kind of check. The compilers of the survey give details of 250 persons who mistook the broadcast for a news bulletin. It appears that over a third of them attempted no kind of verification; as soon as they heard that the end of the world was coming, they accepted it uncritically. A few imagined that it was really a German or Japanese invasion, but the majority believed in the Martians, and this included people who had only heard of the 'invasion' from neighbours, and even a few who had started off with the knowledge that they were listening to a play. [. . .]

The survey does not reveal any single all-embracing explanation of the panic. All it establishes is that the people most likely to be affected were the poor, the ill-educated and, above all, people who were economically insecure or had unhappy private lives. The evident connection between personal unhappiness and readiness to believe the incredible is its most interesting discovery. Remarks like 'Everything is so upset in the world that anything might happen,' or 'So long as everybody was going to die, it was all right,' are surprisingly common in the answers to the questionnaire.

People who have been out of work or on the verge of bankruptcy for ten years may be actually relieved to hear of the approaching end of civilisation. It is a similar frame of mind that has induced whole nations to fling themselves into the arms of a Saviour.

'One of the easiest pastimes in the world is debunking Democracy.'

from 'Fascism and Democracy',
The Left News, February 1941

ONE OF THE EASIEST pastimes in the world is debunking Democracy. In this country one is hardly obliged to bother any longer with the merely reactionary arguments against popular rule, but during the last twenty years 'bourgeois' Democracy has been much more subtly attacked by both Fascists and Communists, and it is highly significant that these seeming enemies have both attacked it on the same grounds. It is true that the Fascists, with their bolder methods of propaganda, also use when it suits them the aristocratic argument that Democracy 'brings the worst men to the top,' but the basic contention of all apologists of totalitarianism is that Democracy is a fraud. It is supposed to be no more than a cover-up for the rule of small handfuls of rich men. This is not altogether false, and still less is it obviously false; on the contrary, there is more to be said for it than against it. A sixteen-year-old schoolboy can attack Democracy much better than he can defend it. And one cannot answer him unless one knows the anti-democratic 'case' and is willing to admit the large measure of truth it contains.

To begin with, it is always urged against 'bourgeois' Democracy that it is negatived by economic inequality. What is the use of political liberty, so called, to a man who works 12 hours a day for £3 a week? Once in five years he may get the chance to vote for his favourite party, but for the rest of the time practically every detail of his life is dictated by his employer. And in practice his political life is dictated as well. The monied class can keep all the important ministerial and official jobs in its own hands, and it can work the electoral system in its own favour by bribing the electorate, directly or indirectly. Even when by some mischance a government representing the poorer classes gets into power, the rich can usually blackmail it by threatening to export capital. Most important of all, nearly the whole cultural and intellectual life of the community—newspapers, books, education, films, radio—is controlled by monied men who have the strongest motive to prevent the spread of certain ideas. The citizen of a democratic country is 'conditioned' from birth onwards, less rigidly but not much less effectively than he would be in a totalitarian state.

And there is no certainty that the rule of a privileged class can ever be broken by purely democratic means. In theory a Labour government could come into office with a clear majority and proceed at once to establish socialism by Act of Parliament. In practice the monied classes would rebel, and probably with success, because they would have most of the permanent officials and the key men in the armed forces on their side. Democratic methods are only possible where there is a fairly large basis of agreement between all political parties. There is no strong reason for thinking that any really fundamental change can ever be achieved peacefully.

Again, it is often argued that the whole façade of democracy—freedom of speech and assembly, independent trade unions and so forth—must collapse as soon as the monied classes are no longer in a position to make concessions to their employees. Political 'liberty,' it is said, is simply a bribe, a bloodless substitute for the Gestapo. It is a fact that the countries we call democratic are usually prosperous countries—in most cases they are exploiting cheap coloured labour, directly or indirectly—and also that Democracy as we know it has never existed except in maritime or mountainous countries, i.e. countries which can defend themselves without the need for an enormous standing army. Democracy accompanies, probably demands, favourable conditions of life; it has never flourished in poor and militarised states. Take away England's sheltered position, so it is said, and England will promptly revert to political methods as barbarous as those of

Rumania. Moreover all government, democratic or totalitarian, rests ultimately on force. No government, unless it intends to connive at its own overthrow, can or does show the smallest respect for democratic 'rights' when once it is seriously menaced. A democratic country fighting a desperate war is forced, just as much as an autocracy or a Fascist state, to conscript soldiers, coerce labour, imprison defeatists, suppress seditious newspapers; in other words, it can only save itself from destruction by ceasing to be democratic. The things it is supposed to be fighting for are always scrapped as soon as the fighting starts.

That, roughly summarised, is the case against 'bourgeois' Democracy, advanced by Fascists and Communists alike, though with differences of emphasis. At every point one has got to admit that it contains much truth. And yet why is it that it is ultimately false — for everyone bred in a democratic country knows quasi-instinctively that there is something wrong with the whole of this line of argument?

What is wrong with this familiar debunking

of Democracy is that it cannot explain the whole of the facts. The actual differences in social atmosphere and political behaviour between country and country are far greater than can be explained by any theory which writes off laws, customs, traditions, etc. as mere 'superstructure.' On paper it is very simple to demonstrate that Democracy is 'just the same as' (or 'just as bad as') totalitarianism. There are concentration camps in Germany; but then there are concentration camps in India. Jews are persecuted wherever fascism reigns; but what about the colour laws in South Africa? Intellectual honesty is a crime in any totalitarian country; but even in England it is not exactly profitable to speak and write the truth. These parallels can be extended indefinitely. But the implied argument all along the line is that a difference of degree is not a difference. It is quite true, for instance, that there is political persecution in democratic countries. The question is how much. How many refugees have fled from Britain, or from the whole of the British Empire, during the past seven years?

And how many from Germany? How many people personally known to you have been beaten with rubber truncheons or forced to swallow pints of castor oil? How dangerous do you feel it to be to go into the nearest pub and express your opinion that this is a capitalist war and we ought to stop fighting? Can you point to anything in recent British or American history that compares with the June Purge, the Russian Trotskyist trials, the pogrom that followed vom Rath's assassination? Could an article equivalent to the one I am writing be printed in any totalitarian country, red, brown or black?

INTELLECTUAL HONESTY is a

CRIME

in any totalitarian country; but

even in England it is not exactly

profitable to speak and write the

TRUTH.

'Till recently it was thought proper to pretend that all human beings are very much alike'

from *The Lion and the Unicorn* (February 1941)

As I WRITE, highly civilized human beings are flying overhead, trying to kill me. They do not feel any enmity against me as [an] individual, nor I against them. They are 'only doing their duty', as the saying goes. Most of them, I have no doubt, are kind-hearted law-abiding men who would never dream of committing murder in private life. On the other hand, if one of them succeeds in blowing me to pieces with a well-placed bomb, he will never sleep any the worse for it. He is serving his country, which has the power to absolve him from evil.

One cannot see the modern world as it is unless one recognizes the overwhelming strength of patriotism, national loyalty. In certain circumstances it can break down, at certain levels of civilization it does not exist, but as a positive force there is nothing to set beside it. Christianity and international Socialism are as weak as straw in comparison with it. Hitler and Mussolini rose to power in their own countries very largely because they could grasp this fact and their opponents could not.

Also, one must admit that the divisions between nation and nation are founded on real differences of outlook. Till recently it was thought proper to pretend that all human beings are very much alike, but in fact anyone able to use his eyes knows that the average of human behaviour differs enormously from country to country. Things that could happen in one country could not happen in another. Hitler's June Purge, for instance, could not have happened in England. And, as western peoples go, the English are very highly differentiated. There is a sort of backhanded admission of this in the dislike which nearly all foreigners feel for our national way of life. Few Europeans can endure living in England, and even Americans often feel more at home in Europe.

When you come back to England from any foreign country, you have immediately the sensation of breathing a different air. Even in the first few minutes dozens of small things conspire to give you this feeling. The beer is bitterer, the coins are heavier, the grass is greener, the advertisements are more blatant. The crowds in the big towns, with their mild knobby faces, their bad teeth and gentle manners, are different from a European crowd. Then the vastness of England swallows you up, and you lose for a while your feeling that the whole nation has a single identifiable character. Are there really such things as nations? Are we not 46 million individuals, all different? And the diversity of it, the chaos! The clatter of clogs in the Lancashire mill towns, the to-and-fro of the lorries on the Great North Road, the queues outside the Labour Exchanges, the rattle of pin-tables in the Soho pubs, the old maids biking to Holy Communion through the mists of the autumn mornings—all these are not only fragments, but characteristic fragments, of the English scene. How can one make a pattern out of this muddle?

But talk to foreigners, read foreign books or newspapers, and you are brought back to the same thought. Yes, there is something distinctive and recognizable in English civilization. It is a culture as individual as that of Spain. It is somehow bound up with solid breakfasts and gloomy Sundays, smoky towns and winding roads, green fields and red pillar-boxes. It has a flavour of its own. Moreover it is continuous, it stretches into the future and the past, there is something in it that persists, as in a living creature. What can the England of 1940 have in common with the England of 1840? But then, what have you in common with the child of five whose photograph your mother keeps on the mantelpiece? Nothing, except that you happen to be the same person.

[. . .] In England all the boasting and flag-wagging, the 'Rule Britannia' stuff, is done by small minorities. The patriotism of the common people is not vocal or even conscious. They do not retain among their historical memories the name of a single military victory. English literature, like other literatures, is full of battle-poems, but it is worth noticing that the ones that have won for themselves a kind of popularity are always a tale of disasters and retreats. There is no popular poem about Trafalgar or Waterloo, for instance. Sir John Moore's army at Corunna, fighting a desperate rear-guard action before escaping overseas (just like Dunkirk!) has more appeal than a brilliant victory. The most stirring battle-poem in English is about a brigade of cavalry which charged in the wrong direction. And of the last war, the four names which have really engraved themselves on the popular memory are Mons, Ypres, Gallipoli and Passchendaele, every time a disaster. The names of the great battles that finally broke the German armies are simply unknown to the general public.

The reason why the English anti-militarism disgusts foreign observers is that it ignores the existence of the British Empire. It looks like sheer hypocrisy. After all, the English have absorbed a quarter of the earth and held on to it by means of a huge navy. How dare they then turn round and say that war is wicked?

It is quite true that the English are hypocritical about their Empire. In the working class this hypocrisy takes the form of not knowing that the Empire exists. But their dislike of standing armies is a perfectly sound instinct. A navy employs comparatively few people, and it is an external weapon which cannot affect home politics directly. Military dictatorships exist everywhere, but there is no such thing as a naval dictatorship. What English people of nearly all classes loathe from the bottom of their hearts is the swaggering officer type, the jingle of spurs and the crash of boots. Decades before Hitler was ever heard of, the word 'Prussian' had much the same significance in England as 'Nazi' has to-day. So deep does this feeling go that for a hundred years past the officers of the British Army, in peace-time, have always worn civilian clothes when off duty.

One rapid but fairly sure guide to the social atmosphere of a country is the parade-step of its army. A military parade is really a kind of ritual dance, something like a ballet, expressing a certain philosophy of life. The goose-step, for instance, is one of the most horrible sights in the world, far more terrifying than a dive-bomber. It is simply an affirmation of naked power; contained in it, quite consciously and intentionally, is the vision of a boot crashing down on a face. Its ugliness is part of its essence, for what it is saying is 'Yes, I am ugly, and you daren't laugh at me', like the bully who makes faces at his victim. Why is the goose-step not used in England? There are, heaven knows, plenty of army officers who would be only too glad to introduce some such thing. It is not used because the people in the street would laugh. Beyond a certain point, military display is only possible in countries where the common people dare not laugh at the army. The Italians adopted the goose-step at about the time when Italy passed definitely under German control, and, as one would expect, they do it less well than the Germans. The Vichy government, if it survives, is bound to introduce a stiffer parade-ground discipline into what is left of the French army. In the British army the drill is rigid and complicated, full of memories of the eighteenth century, but without definite swagger; the march is merely a formalized walk. It belongs to a society which is ruled by the sword, no doubt, but a sword which must never be taken out of the scabbard.

And yet the gentleness of English civilization is mixed up with barbarities and anachronisms. Our criminal law is as out of date as the muskets in the Tower. Over against the Nazi Storm Trooper you have got to set that typically English figure, the hanging judge, some gouty old bully with his mind rooted in the nineteenth century, handing out savage sentences. In England people are still hanged by the neck and flogged with the cat o' nine tails. Both of these punishments are obscene as well as cruel, but there has never been any genuinely popular outcry against them. People accept them (and Dartmoor, and Borstal) almost as they accept the weather. They are part of 'the law', which is assumed to be unalterable.

Here one comes upon an all-important English trait: the respect for constitutionalism and legality, the belief in 'the law' as something above the State and above the individual, something which is cruel and stupid, of course, but at any rate incorruptible.

It is not that anyone imagines the law to be just. Everyone knows that there is one law for the rich and another for the poor. But no one accepts the implications of this, everyone takes it for granted that the law, such as it is, will be respected, and feels a sense of outrage when it is not. Remarks like 'They can't run me in; I haven't done anything wrong', or 'They can't do that; it's against the law', are part of the atmosphere of England. The professed enemies of society have this feeling as strongly as anyone else. One sees it in prison-books like Wilfred Macartney's *Walls Have Mouths* or Jim Phelan's *Jail Journey*, in the solemn idiocies that take place at the trials of Conscientious Objectors, in letters to the papers from eminent Marxist professors, pointing out that this or that is a 'miscarriage of British justice'. Everyone believes in his heart that the law can be, ought to be, and, on the whole, will be impartially administered. The totalitarian idea that there is no such thing as law, there is only power, has never taken root. Even the intelligentsia have only accepted it in theory.

An illusion can become a half-truth, a mask can alter the expression of a face. The familiar arguments to the effect that democracy is 'just the same as' or 'just as bad as' totalitarianism never take account of this fact. All such arguments boil down to saying that half a loaf is the same as no bread. In England such concepts as justice, liberty and objective truth are still believed in. They may be illusions, but they are very powerful illusions. The belief in them influences conduct, national life is different because of them. In proof of which, look about you. Where are the rubber truncheons, where is the castor oil? The sword is still in the scabbard, and while it stays there corruption cannot go beyond a certain point. The English electoral system, for instance, is an all-but open fraud. In a dozen obvious ways it is gerrymandered in the interest of the moneyed class. But until some deep change has occurred in the public mind, it cannot become completely corrupt.

You do not arrive at the polling booth to find men with revolvers telling you which way to vote, nor are the votes miscounted, nor is there any direct bribery. Even hypocrisy is a powerful safeguard. The hanging judge, that evil old man in scarlet robe and horsehair wig, whom nothing short of dynamite will ever teach what century he is living in, but who will at any rate interpret the law according to the books and will in no circumstances take a money bribe, is one of the symbolic figures of England. He is a symbol of the strange mixture of reality and illusion, democracy and privilege, humbug and decency, the subtle network of compromises, by which the nation keeps itself in its familiar shape.

In England such concepts as justice, liberty and objective truth are still believed in. They may be

ILLUSIONS,

BUT THEY ARE
VERY POWERFUL

ILLUSIONS.

'Is the English press honest or dishonest?'

from *The Lion and the Unicorn* (February 1941)

AT THIS MOMENT, after a year of war, news-papers and pamphlets abusing the Government, praising the enemy and clamouring for surrender are being sold on the streets, almost without interference. And this is less from a respect for freedom of speech than from a simple perception that these things don't matter. It is safe to let a paper like *Peace News* be sold, because it is certain that ninety-five per cent of the population will never want to read it. The nation is bound together by an invisible chain. At any normal time the ruling class will rob, mismanage, sabotage, lead us into the muck; but let popular opinion really make itself heard, let them get a tug from below that they cannot avoid feeling, and it is difficult for them not to respond. The left-wing writers who denounce the whole of the ruling class as 'pro-Fascist' are grossly over-simplifying. Even among the inner clique of politicians who brought us to our present pass, it is doubtful whether there were any conscious traitors. The corruption that happens in England is seldom of that kind. Nearly always it is more in the nature of self-deception, of the right hand not knowing what the left hand doeth. And being unconscious, it is limited. One sees this at its most obvious in the English Press. Is the English press honest or dishonest? At normal times it is deeply dishonest. All the papers that matter live off their advertisements, and the advertisers exercise an indirect censorship over news. Yet I do not suppose there is one paper in England that can be straightforwardly bribed with hard cash. In the France of the Third Republic all but a very few of the newspapers could notoriously be bought over the counter like so many pounds of cheese. Public life in England has never been openly scandalous. It has not reached the pitch of disintegration at which humbug can be dropped.

England is not the jewelled isle of Shakespeare's much-quoted passage, nor is it the inferno depicted by Dr. Goebbels. More than either it resembles a family, a rather stuffy Victorian family, with not many black sheep in it but with all its cupboards bursting with skeletons. It has rich relations who have to be kowtowed to and poor relations who are horribly sat upon, and there is a deep conspiracy of silence about the source of the family income. It is a family in which the young are generally thwarted and most of the power is in the hands of irresponsible uncles and bedridden aunts. Still, it is a family. It has its private language and its common memories, and at the approach of an enemy it closes its ranks. A family with the wrong members in control—that, perhaps, is as near as one can come to describing England in a phrase.

'This is the most truthful war that has been fought in modern times.'

from 'London Letter', 15 April 1941;
Partisan Review, July–August 1941

AS TO ACCURACY OF NEWS, I believe this is the most truthful war that has been fought in modern times. Of course one only sees enemy newspapers very rarely, but in our own papers there is certainly nothing to compare with the frightful lies that were told on both sides in 1914–18 or in the Spanish civil war. I believe that the radio, especially in countries where listening-in to foreign broadcasts is not forbidden, is making large-scale lying more and more difficult. The Germans have now sunk the British navy several times over in their published pronouncements, but don't otherwise seem to have lied much about major events. When things are going badly our own government lies in a rather stupid way, withholding information and being vaguely optimistic, but generally has to come out with the truth within a few days. I have it on very good authority that reports of air-battles, etc., issued by the Air Ministry are substantially truthful, though of course favourably coloured. As to the other two fighting services I can't speak. I doubt whether labour troubles are really fully reported. News of a large-scale strike would probably never be suppressed, but I think you can take it that there is a strong tendency to pipe down on labour friction, and also on the discontent caused by billeting, evacuation, separation allowances for soldiers' wives, etc., etc. Debates in Parliament are probably not misrepresented in the press, but with a House full of deadheads they are growing less and less interesting and only about four newspapers now give them prominence.

Propaganda enters into our lives more than it did a year ago, but not so grossly as it might. The flag-waving and Hun-hating is absolutely nothing to what it was in 1914–18, but it is growing. I think the majority opinion would now be that we are fighting the German people and not merely the Nazis. Vansittart's hate-Germany pamphlet, *Black Record*, sold like hot cakes. It is idle to pretend that this is simply something peculiar to the bourgeoisie. There have been very ugly manifestations of it among the common people. Still, as wars go, there has been remarkably little hatred so far, at any rate in this country. Nor is 'anti-fascism,' of the kind that was fashionable during the Popular Front period, a strong force yet. The English people have never caught up with that. Their war morale depends more on old-fashioned patriotism, unwillingness to be governed by foreigners, and simple inability to grasp when they are in danger.

I believe that the B.B.C., in spite of the stupidity of its foreign propaganda and the unbearable voices of its announcers, is very truthful. It is generally regarded here as more reliable than the press. The movies seem almost unaffected by the war, i.e., in technique and subject-matter. They go on and on with the same treacly rubbish, and when they do touch on politics they are years behind the popular press and decades behind the average book.

'Art and propaganda are never quite separable'

'Literary Criticism II: Tolstoy and Shakespeare',
broadcast 7 May 1941; *The Listener*, 5 June 1941

LAST WEEK I pointed out that art and propaganda are never quite separable, and that what are supposed to be purely aesthetic judgments are always corrupted to some extent by moral or political or religious loyalties. And I added that in times of trouble, like the last ten years, in which no thinking person can ignore what is happening round him or avoid taking sides, these underlying loyalties are pushed nearer to the surface of consciousness. Criticism becomes more and more openly partisan, and even the pretence of detachment becomes very difficult. But one cannot infer from that that there is no such thing as an aesthetic judgment, that every work of art is simply and solely a political pamphlet and can be judged only as such. If we reason like that we lead our minds into a blind alley in which certain large and obvious facts become inexplicable. And in illustration of this I want to examine one of the greatest pieces of moral, non-aesthetic criticism—anti-aesthetic criticism, one might say—that have ever been written: Tolstoy's essay on Shakespeare.

Towards the end of his life Tolstoy wrote a terrific attack on Shakespeare, purporting to show not only that Shakespeare was not the great man he was claimed to be, but that he was a writer entirely without merit, one of the worst and most contemptible writers the world has ever seen. This essay caused tremendous indignation at the time, but I doubt whether it was ever satisfactorily answered. What is more, I shall point out that in the main it was unanswerable. Part of what Tolstoy says is strictly true, and parts of it are too much a matter of personal opinion to be worth arguing about. I do not mean, of course, that there is no detail in the essay which could be answered. Tolstoy contradicts himself several times; the fact that he is dealing with a foreign language makes him misunderstand a great deal, and I think there is little doubt that his hatred and jealousy of Shakespeare make him resort to a certain amount of falsification, or at least wilful blindness. But all that is beside the point. In the main what Tolstoy says is justified after its fashion, and at the time it probably acted as a useful corrective to the silly adulation of Shakespeare that was then fashionable. The answer to it is less in anything I can say than in certain things that Tolstoy is forced to say himself.

Tolstoy's main contention is that Shakespeare is a trivial, shallow writer, with no coherent philosophy, no thoughts or ideas worth bothering about, no interest in social or religious problems, no grasp of character or probability, and, in so far as he could be said to have a definable attitude at all, with a cynical, immoral, worldly outlook on life. He accuses him of patching his plays together without caring twopence for credibility, of dealing in fantastic fables and impossible situations, of making all his characters talk in an artificial flowery language completely unlike that of real life. He also accuses him of thrusting anything and everything into his plays—soliloquies, scraps of ballads, discussions, vulgar jokes and so forth—without stopping to think whether they had anything to do with the plot, and also of taking for granted the immoral power-politics and unjust social distinctions of the times he lived in. Briefly, he accuses him of being a hasty, slovenly writer, a man of doubtful morals, and, above all, of not being a *thinker*.

Now, a good deal of this could be contradicted. It is not true, in the sense implied by Tolstoy, that Shakespeare is an immoral writer. His moral code might be different from Tolstoy's, but he very definitely has a moral code, which is apparent all through his work. He is much more of a moralist than, for instance, Chaucer or Boccaccio. He also is not such a fool as Tolstoy tries to make out. At moments, incidentally, one might say, he shows a vision which goes far beyond his time. In this connection I would like to draw attention to the piece of criticism which Karl Marx—who, unlike Tolstoy, admired Shakespeare—wrote on 'Timon of Athens'. But once again, what Tolstoy says is true on the whole. Shakespeare is not a thinker, and the critics who claimed that he was one of the great philosophers of the world were talking nonsense. His thoughts are simply a jumble, a rag-bag. He was like most Englishmen in having a code of conduct but no world-view, no philosophical faculty. Again, it is quite true that Shakespeare cares very little about probability and seldom bothers to make his characters coherent. As we know, he usually stole his plots from other people and hastily made them up into plays, often introducing absurdities and inconsistencies that were not present in the original. Now and again, when he happens to have got hold of a foolproof plot—'Macbeth', for instance—his characters are reasonably consistent, but in many cases they are forced into actions which are completely incredible by any ordinary standard. Many of his plays have not even the sort of credibility that belongs to a fairy story. In any case we have no evidence that he himself took them seriously, except as a means of livelihood. In his sonnets he never even refers to his plays as part of literary achievement, and only once mentions in a rather shamefaced way that he has been an actor. So far Tolstoy is justified. The claim that Shakespeare was a profound thinker, setting forth a coherent philosophy in plays that were technically perfect and full of subtle psychological observation, is ridiculous.

Only, what has Tolstoy achieved? By this furious attack he ought to have demolished Shakespeare altogether, and he evidently believes that he has done so. From the time when Tolstoy's essay was written, or at any rate from the time when it began to be widely read, Shakespeare's reputation ought to have withered away. The lovers of Shakespeare ought to have seen that their idol had been debunked, that in fact he had no merits, and they ought to have ceased forthwith to take any pleasure in him. But that did not happen. Shakespeare is demolished, and yet somehow he remains standing. So far from his being forgotten as the result of Tolstoy's attack, it is the attack itself that has been almost forgotten. Although Tolstoy is a popular writer in England, both the translations of this essay are out of print, and I had to search all over London before running one to earth in a museum.

It appears, therefore, that though Tolstoy can explain away nearly everything about Shakespeare, there is one thing that he cannot explain away, and that is his popularity. He himself is aware of this, and greatly puzzled by it. I said earlier that the answer to Tolstoy really lies in something he himself is obliged to say. He asks himself how it is that this bad, stupid and immoral writer Shakespeare is everywhere admired, and finally he can only explain it as a sort of world-wide conspiracy to pervert the truth. Or it is a sort of collective hallucination—a hypnosis, he calls it—by which everyone except Tolstoy himself is taken in. As to how this conspiracy or delusion began, he is obliged to set it down to the machinations of certain German critics at the beginning of the nineteenth century. They started telling the wicked lie that Shakespeare is a good writer, and no one since has had the courage to contradict them. Now, one need not spend very long over a theory of this kind. It is nonsense. The enormous majority of the people who have enjoyed watching Shakespeare's plays have never been influenced by any German critics, directly or indirectly. For Shakespeare's popularity is real enough, and it is a popularity that extends to ordinary, by no means bookish people. From his lifetime onwards he has been a stage favourite in England, and he is popular not only in the English-speaking countries but in most of Europe and parts of Asia. Almost as I speak the Soviet Government are celebrating the three hundred and twenty-fifth anniversary of his death, and in Ceylon I once saw a play of his being performed in some language of which I did not know a single word. One must conclude that there is something good—something durable—in Shakespeare which millions of ordinary people can appreciate, though Tolstoy happened to be unable to do so. He can survive exposure of the fact that he is a confused thinker whose plays are full of improbabilities. He can no more be debunked by such methods than you can destroy a flower by preaching a sermon at it.

And that, I think, tells one a little more about

something I referred to last week: the frontiers of art and propaganda. It shows one the limitation of any criticism that is solely a criticism of subject and of meaning. Tolstoy criticises Shakespeare not as a poet, but as a thinker and a teacher, and along those lines he has no difficulty in demolishing him. And yet all that he says is irrelevant; Shakespeare is completely unaffected. Not only his reputation but the pleasure we take in him remain just the same as before. Evidently a poet is more than a thinker and a teacher, though he has to be that as well. Every piece of writing has its propaganda aspect, and yet in any book or play or poem or what-not that is to endure there has to be a residuum of something that simply is not affected by its moral or meaning—a residuum of something we can only call art. Within certain limits, bad thought and bad morals can be good literature. If so great a man as Tolstoy could not demonstrate the contrary, I doubt whether anyone else can either.

'The first thing that we ask of a writer is that
he shan't tell lies'

'Literary Criticism IV: Literature and Totalitarianism',
broadcast 21 May 1941; typescript

IN THESE WEEKLY TALKS I have been speaking on criticism, which, when all is said and
done, is not part of the main stream of literature. A vigorous literature can exist almost
without criticism and the critical spirit, as it did
in nineteenth-century England. But there is a
reason why, at this particular moment, the problems involved in any serious criticism cannot be
ignored. I said at the beginning of my first talk
that this is not a critical age. It is an age of partisanship and not of detachment, an age in which
it is especially difficult to see literary merit in
a book whose conclusions you disagree with.
Politics—politics in the most general sense—
have invaded literature to an extent that doesn't
normally happen, and this has brought to the
surface of our consciousness the struggle that
always goes on between the individual and the

community. It is when one considers the difficulty of writing honest, unbiassed criticism in a time like ours that one begins to grasp the nature of the threat that hangs over the whole of literature in the coming age.

We live in an age in which the autonomous individual is ceasing to exist — or perhaps one ought to say, in which the individual is ceasing to have the illusion of being autonomous. Now, in all that we say about literature, and above all in all that we say about criticism, we instinctively take the autonomous individual for granted. The whole of modern European literature — I am speaking of the literature of the past four hundred years — is built on the concept of intellectual honesty, or, if you like to put it that way, on Shakespeare's maxim, 'To thine own self be true'. The first thing that we ask of a writer is that he shan't tell lies, that he shall say what he really thinks, what he really feels. The worst thing we can say about a work of art is that it is insincere. And this is even truer of criticism than of creative literature, in which a certain amount of posing and mannerism and even a certain amount of downright humbug, doesn't matter so long as the writer has a certain fundamental sincerity. Modern literature is essentially an individual thing. It is either the truthful expression of what one man thinks and feels, or it is nothing.

[. . .] Totalitarianism has abolished freedom of thought to an extent unheard of in any previous age. And it is important to realise that its control of thought is not only negative, but positive. It not only forbids you to express— even to *think*—certain thoughts but it dictates what you *shall* think, it creates an ideology for you, it tries to govern your emotional life as well as setting up a code of conduct. And as far as possible it isolates you from the outside world, it shuts you up in an artificial universe in which you have no standards of comparison. The totalitarian state tries, at any rate, to control the thoughts and emotions of its subjects at least as completely as it controls their actions.

The question that is important for us is, can literature survive in such an atmosphere? I think one must answer shortly that it cannot. If totalitarianism becomes worldwide and permanent, what we have known as literature must come to an end. And it won't do — as may appear plausible at first — to say that what will come to an end is merely the literature of post-Renaissance Europe. I believe that literature of every kind, from the epic poem to the critical essay, is menaced by the attempt of the modern state to control the emotional life of the individual. The people who deny this usually put forward two arguments. They say, first of all, that the so-called liberty which has existed during the last few hundred years was merely a reflection of economic anarchy, and in any case largely an illusion. And they also point out that good literature, better than anything that we can produce now, was produced in past ages, when thought was hardly freer than it is in Germany or Russia at this moment. Now this is true so far as it goes. It's true, for instance, that literature could exist in medieval Europe, when thought was under rigid control — chiefly the control of the Church — and you were liable to be burnt alive for uttering a very small heresy. The dogmatic control of the Church didn't prevent, for instance, Chaucer's Canterbury Tales from being written. It's also true that medieval literature, and medieval art generally, was less an individual and more a communal thing than it is now. The English ballads, for example, probably can't be attributed to any individual at all. They were probably composed communally, as I have seen ballads being composed in Eastern countries quite recently. Evidently the anarchic liberty which has characterised the Europe of the last few hundred years, the sort of atmosphere in which there are no fixed standards whatever, isn't necessary, perhaps isn't even an advantage, to literature. Good literature can be created within a fixed framework of thought.

But there are several vital differences between totalitarianism and all the orthodoxies of the past, either in Europe or in the East. The most important is that the orthodoxies of the past didn't change, or at least didn't change rapidly. In medieval Europe the Church dictated what you should believe, but at least it allowed you to retain the same beliefs from birth to death. It didn't tell you to believe one thing on Monday and another on Tuesday. And the same is more or less true of any orthodox Christian, Hindu, Buddhist or Moslem today. In a sense his thoughts are circumscribed, but he passes his whole life within the same framework of thought. His emotions aren't tampered with. Now, with totalitarianism exactly the opposite is true. The peculiarity of the totalitarian state is that though it controls thought, it doesn't fix it. It sets up unquestionable dogmas, and it alters them from day to day. It needs the dogmas, because it needs absolute obedience from its subjects, but it can't avoid the changes, which are dictated by the needs of power politics. It declares itself infallible, and at the same time it attacks the very concept of objective truth. To take a crude, obvious example, every German up to September 1939 had to regard Russian Bolshevism with horror and aversion, and since September 1939 he has had to regard it with admiration and affection. If Russia and Germany go to war, as they may well do within the next few years,* another equally violent change will have to take place. The German's emotional life, his loves and hatreds, are expected, when necessary, to reverse themselves overnight. I hardly need to point out the effect of this kind of thing upon literature. For writing is largely a matter of feeling, which can't always be controlled from outside. It is easy to pay lip-service to the orthodoxy of the moment, but writing of any consequence can only be produced when a man feels the truth of what he is saying; without that, the creative impulse is lacking. All the evidence we have suggests that the sudden emotional changes which totalitarianism demands of its followers are psychologically impossible. And that is the chief reason why I suggest that if totalitarianism triumphs throughout the world, literature as we have known it is at an end. And in fact, totalitarianism does seem to have had that effect so far. In Italy literature has been crip-

---

* Publisher's note: In fact the Axis powers invaded the USSR only a month after this broadcast.

pled, and in Germany it seems almost to have ceased. The most characteristic activity of the Nazis is burning books. And even in Russia the literary renaissance we once expected hasn't happened, and the most promising Russian writers show a marked tendency to commit suicide or disappear into prison.

[. . .] Whoever feels the value of literature, whoever sees the central part it plays in the development of human history, must also see the life and death necessity of resisting totalitarianism, whether it is imposed on us from without or from within.

'The most one can truly say for Stalin is that probably he is individually sincere'

from War-time Diary, 3 July 1941

Stalin's broadcast speech is a direct return to the Popular Front, defence of democracy line, and in effect a complete contradiction of all that he and his followers have been saying for the past two years. It was nevertheless a magnificent fighting speech, just the right counterpart to Churchill's, and made it clear that no compromise is intended, at any rate at this moment. Passages in it seemed to imply that a big retreat is contemplated, however. Britain and the U.S.A. referred to in friendly terms and more or less as allies, though apparently no formal alliance exists as yet. Ribbentrop and Co. spoken of as 'cannibals', which Pravda *has also been calling them. Apparently one reason for the queer phraseology that translated Russian speeches often have is that Russian contains so large a vocabulary of abusive words that English equivalents do not exist.*

One could not have a better example of the moral

and emotional shallowness of our time, than the fact that we are now all more or less pro-Stalin. This disgusting murderer is temporarily on our side, and so the purges, etc., are suddenly forgotten. So also with Franco, Mussolini, etc., should they ultimately come over to us. The most one can truly say for Stalin is that probably he is individually sincere, as his followers cannot be, for his endless changes of front are at any rate his own decision. It is a case of 'when Father turns we all turn', and Father presumably turns because the spirit moves him.

'One of the worst things about democratic society in the last twenty years has been the difficulty of any straight talking or thinking.'

from 'Culture and Democracy', 22 November 1941

ONE OF THE WORST things about democratic society in the last twenty years has been the difficulty of any straight talking or thinking. Let me take one important fact, I might say the basic fact about our social structure. That is, that it is founded on cheap coloured labour. As the world is now constituted, we are all standing on the backs of half-starved Asiatic coolies. The standard of living of the British working class has been and is artificially high because it is based on a parasitic economy. The working class is as much involved in the exploitation of coloured labour as anybody else, but so far as I know, nowhere in the British Press in the last twenty years—at any rate in no part of the Press likely to get wide attention—do you find any clear admission of that fact or any straight talking about it. In the last twenty years there were really two policies open to us as a nation living on coloured labour. One was to say frankly: We are the master-race—and remember, that is how Hitler talks to his people, because he is a totalitarian leader and can speak frankly on certain subjects—we are the master-race, we live by exploiting inferior races, let's all get together and squeeze as much out of them as we can. That was one policy; that was what, shall we say, *The Times* ought to have said if it had had the guts. It didn't say it. The other possible policy was to say something like this: We cannot go on exploiting the world for ever, we must do justice to the Indians, the Chinese and all the rest of them, and since our standard of living is artificially high and the process of adjustment is bound to be painful and difficult, we must be ready to lower that standard of living for the time being. Also, since powerful influences will be at work to prevent the underdog from getting his rights, we must arm ourselves against the coming international civil war, instead of simply agitating for higher wages and shorter hours. That is what, for instance, the *Daily Herald* would have said if it had had the guts. Once again, nowhere will you find anything like that in plain words. You simply couldn't say that kind of thing in newspapers which had to live off their circulation and off advertisements for consumption goods.

'All propaganda is lies'

from War-time Diary, 14 March 1942

All propaganda is lies, even when one is telling the truth. I don't think this matters so long as one knows what one is doing, and why.

'Everyone believes in the atrocities of the enemy and disbelieves in those of his own side'

from 'Looking Back on the Spanish War' (1943)

I HAVE LITTLE DIRECT evidence about the atrocities in the Spanish Civil War. I know that some were committed by the Republicans, and far more (they are still continuing) by the Fascists. But what impressed me then, and has impressed me ever since, is that atrocities are believed in or disbelieved in solely on grounds of political predilection. Everyone believes in the atrocities of the enemy and disbelieves in those of his own side, without ever bothering to examine the evidence. Recently I drew up a table of atrocities during the period between 1918 and the present; there was never a year when atrocities were not occurring somewhere or other, and there was hardly a single case when the Left and the Right believed in the same stories simultaneously. And stranger yet, at any moment the situation can suddenly reverse itself and yesterday's proved-to-the-hilt atrocity story can become a ridiculous lie, merely because the political landscape has changed.

In the present war we are in the curious situation that our 'atrocity campaign' was done largely before the war started, and done mostly by the Left, the people who normally pride themselves on their incredulity. In the same period the Right, the atrocity-mongers of 1914–18, were gazing at Nazi Germany and flatly refusing to see any evil in it. Then as soon as war broke out it was the pro-Nazis of yesterday who were repeating horror-stories, while the anti-Nazis suddenly found themselves doubting whether the Gestapo really existed. Nor was this solely the result of the Russo-German Pact. It was partly because before the war the Left had wrongly believed that Britain and Germany would never fight and were therefore able to be anti-German and anti-British simultaneously; partly also because official war-propaganda, with its disgusting hypocrisy and self-righteousness, always tends to make thinking people sympathise with the enemy. Part of the price we paid for the systematic lying of 1914–18 was the exaggerated pro-German reaction which followed. During the years 1918–33 you were hooted at in left-wing circles if you suggested that Germany bore even a fraction of responsibility for the war. In all the denunciations of Versailles I listened to during those years I don't think I ever once heard the question, 'What would have happened if Germany had won?' even mentioned, let alone discussed. So also with atrocities. The truth, it is felt, becomes untruth when your enemy utters it. Recently I noticed that the very people who swallowed any and every horror story about the Japanese in Nanking in 1937 refused to believe exactly the same stories about Hong Kong in 1942. There was even a tendency to feel that the Nanking atrocities had become, as it were, retrospectively untrue because the British Government now drew attention to them.

But unfortunately the truth about atrocities is far worse than that they are lied about and made into propaganda. The truth is that they happen. The fact often adduced as a reason for scepticism—that the same horror stories come up in war after war—merely makes it rather more likely that these stories are true. Evidently they are widespread fantasies, and war provides an opportunity of putting them into practice. Also, although it has ceased to be fashionable to say so, there is little question that what one may roughly call the 'whites' commit far more and worse atrocities than the 'reds'. There is not the slightest doubt, for instance, about the behaviour of the Japanese in China. Nor is there much doubt about the long tale of Fascist outrages during the last ten years in Europe. The volume of testimony is enormous, and a respectable proportion of it comes from the German press and radio. These things really happened, that is the thing to keep one's eye on. They happened even though Lord Halifax said they happened. The raping and butchering in Chinese cities, the tortures in the cellars of the Gestapo, the elderly Jewish professors flung into cesspools, the machine-gunning of refugees along the Spanish roads—they all happened, and they did not happen any the less because the *Daily Telegraph* has suddenly found out about them when it is five years too late.

'In Spain, for the first time, I saw newspaper reports which did not bear any relation to the facts'

from 'Looking Back on the Spanish War' (1943)

THE STRUGGLE FOR POWER between the Spanish Republican parties is an unhappy, far-off thing which I have no wish to revive at this date. I only mention it in order to say: believe nothing, or next to nothing, of what you read about internal affairs on the Government side. It is all, from whatever source, party propaganda—that is to say, lies. The broad truth about the war is simple enough. The Spanish bourgeoisie saw their chance of crushing the labour movement, and took it, aided by the Nazis and by the forces of reaction all over the world. It is doubtful whether more than that will ever be established.

I remember saying once to Arthur Koestler, 'History stopped in 1936,' at which he nodded in immediate understanding. We were both thinking of totalitarianism in general, but more particularly of the Spanish Civil War. Early in life I had noticed that no event is ever correctly reported in a newspaper, but in Spain, for the first time, I saw newspaper reports which did not bear any relation to the facts, not even the relationship which is implied in an ordinary lie. I saw great battles reported where there had been no fighting, and complete silence where hundreds of men had been killed. I saw troops who had fought bravely denounced as cowards and traitors, and others who had never seen a shot fired hailed as the heroes of imaginary victories; and I saw newspapers in London retailing these lies and eager intellectuals building emotional superstructures over events that had never happened. I saw, in fact, history being written not in terms of what happened but of what ought to have happened according to various 'party lines'. Yet in a way, horrible as all this was, it was unimportant. It concerned secondary issues—namely, the struggle for power between the Comintern and the Spanish left-wing parties, and the efforts of the Russian Government to prevent revolution in Spain. But the broad picture of the war which the Spanish Government presented to the world was not untruthful. The main issues were what it said they were. But as for the Fascists and their backers, how could they come even as near to the truth as that? How could they possibly mention their real aims? Their version of the war was pure fantasy, and in the circumstances it could not have been otherwise.

The only propaganda line open to the Nazis and Fascists was to represent themselves as Christian patriots saving Spain from a Russian dictatorship. This involved pretending that life in Government Spain was just one long massacre (vide the *Catholic Herald* or the *Daily Mail*—but these were child's play compared with the continental Fascist press), and it involved immensely exaggerating the scale of Russian intervention. Out of the huge pyramid of lies which the Catholic and reactionary press all over the world built up, let me take just one point—the presence in Spain of a Russian army. Devout Franco partisans all believed in this; estimates of its strength went as high as half a million. Now, there was no Russian army in Spain. There may have been a handful of airmen and other technicians, a few hundred at the most, but an army there was not. Some thousands of foreigners who fought in Spain, not to mention millions of Spaniards, were witnesses of this. Well, their testimony made no impression at all upon the Franco propagandists, not one of whom had set foot in Government Spain. Simultaneously these people refused utterly to admit the fact of German or Italian intervention, at the same time as the German and Italian press were openly boasting about the exploits of their 'legionaries'. I have chosen to mention only one point, but in fact the whole of Fascist propaganda about the war was on this level.

This kind of thing is frightening to me, because it often gives me the feeling that the very concept of objective truth is fading out of the world. After all, the chances are that those lies, or at any rate similar lies, will pass into history. How will the history of the Spanish War be written? If Franco remains in power his nominees will write the history books, and (to stick to my chosen point) that Russian army which never existed will become historical fact, and schoolchildren will learn about it generations hence. But suppose Fascism is finally defeated and some kind of democratic government restored in Spain in the fairly near future; even then, how is the history of the war to be written? What kind of records will Franco have left behind him?

Suppose even that the records kept on the Government side are recoverable—even so, how is a true history of the war to be written? For, as I have pointed out already, the Government also dealt extensively in lies. From the anti-Fascist angle one could write a broadly truthful history of the war, but it would be a partisan history, unreliable on every minor point. Yet, after all, some kind of history will be written, and after those who actually remember the war are dead, it will be universally accepted. So for all practical purposes the lie will have become truth.

'What is peculiar to our own age is the abandonment of the idea that history could be truthfully written.'

from 'Looking Back on the Spanish War' (1943)

I KNOW IT IS the fashion to say that most of recorded history is lies anyway. I am willing to believe that history is for the most part inaccurate and biased, but what is peculiar to our own age is the abandonment of the idea that history could be truthfully written. In the past people deliberately lied, or they unconsciously coloured what they wrote, or they struggled after the truth, well knowing that they must make many mistakes; but in each case they believed that 'the facts' existed and were more or less discoverable. And in practice there was always a considerable body of fact which would have been agreed to by almost everyone. If you look up the history of the last war in, for instance, the *Encyclopaedia Britannica*, you will find that a respectable amount of the material is drawn from German sources. A British and a German historian would disagree deeply on many things, even on fundamentals, but there would still be that body of, as it were, neutral fact on which neither would seriously challenge the other. It is just this common basis of agreement, with its implication that human beings are all one species of animal, that totalitarianism destroys. Nazi theory indeed specifically denies that such a thing as 'the truth' exists. There is, for instance, no such thing as 'science'. There is only 'German science', 'Jewish science', etc. The implied objective of this line of thought is a nightmare world in which the Leader, or some ruling clique, controls not only the future but the past. If the Leader says of such and such an event, 'It never happened'—well, it never happened. If he says that two and two are five—well, two and two are five. This prospect frightens me much more than bombs—and after our experiences of the last few years that is not a frivolous statement.

But is it perhaps childish or morbid to terrify

oneself with visions of a totalitarian future? Before writing off the totalitarian world as a nightmare that can't come true, just remember that in 1925 the world of today would have seemed a nightmare that couldn't come true. Against that shifting phantasmagoric world in which black may be white tomorrow and yesterday's weather can be changed by decree, there are in reality only two safeguards. One is that however much you deny the truth, the truth goes on existing, as it were, behind your back, and you consequently can't violate it in ways that impair military efficiency. The other is that so long as some parts of the earth remain unconquered, the liberal tradition can be kept alive. Let Fascism, or possibly even a combination of several Fascisms, conquer the whole world, and those two conditions no longer exist. We in England underrate the danger of this kind of thing, because our traditions and our past security have given us a sentimental belief that it all comes right in the end and the thing you most fear never really happens. Nourished for hundreds of years on a literature in which Right invariably triumphs in the last chapter, we believe half-instinctively that evil always defeats itself in the long run. Pacifism, for instance, is founded largely on this belief. Don't resist evil, and it will somehow destroy itself. But why should it? What evidence is there that it does?

'By making it a penal offence to listen in to Allied broadcasts the Germans have ensured that those broadcasts will be accepted as true.'

from review of *Voices in the Darkness: The Story of the European Radio War* by Tangye Lean,[*]
Tribune, 30 April 1943

ANYONE WHO HAS HAD to do propaganda to 'friendly' countries must envy the European Service of the B.B.C. They are playing on such an easy wicket! People living under a foreign occupation are necessarily hungry for news, and by making it a penal offence to listen in to Allied broadcasts the Germans have ensured that those broadcasts will be accepted as true. There, however, the advantage of the B.B.C.'s European Service ends. If heard it will be be-

---

[*] Publisher's note: Edward Tangye Lean (1911–74), younger brother of the film director David Lean, founder of the Inklings club at Oxford (of which Tolkien and C. S. Lewis were members), and later director of External Broadcasting at the BBC.

lieved, except perhaps in Germany itself, but the difficulty is to be heard at all, and still more, to know what to say. With these difficulties Mr. Tangye Lean's interesting book is largely concerned.

First of all there are the physical and mechanical obstacles. It is never very easy to pick up a foreign station unless one has a fairly good radio set, and every hostile broadcast labours under the enormous disadvantage that its time and wavelength cannot be advertised in the Press. Even in England, where there is no sort of ban on listening, few people have even heard of the German 'freedom' stations such as the New British and the Workers' Challenge. There is also jamming, and above all there is the Gestapo. All over Europe countless people have been imprisoned or sent to concentration camps, and some have been executed, merely for listening to the B.B.C. In countries where surveillance is strict it is only safe to listen on earphones, which may not be available, and in any case the number of workable radio sets is probably declining for want of spare parts.

These physical difficulties themselves lead on to the big and only partly soluble question of what it is safe to say. If your probable audience have got to risk their necks to hear you at all, and have also got to listen, for instance, at midnight in some draughty barn, or with earphones under the bedclothes, is it worth while to attempt propaganda, or must you assume that nothing except 'hard' news is worth broadcasting? Or again, does it pay to do definitely inflammatory propaganda among people whom you are unable to help in a military sense? Or again, is it better from a propaganda point of view to tell the truth or to spread confusing rumours and promise everything to everybody? When it is a case of addressing the enemy and not the conquered populations, the basic question is always whether to cajole or to threaten. Both the British and the German radios have havered between the two policies. So far as truthfulness of news goes the B.B.C. would compare favourably with any non-neutral radio. On the other doubtful points its policy is usually a compromise, sometimes a compromise that makes the worst of both worlds, but there is little question that the stuff which is broadcast to Europe is on a higher intellectual level than what is broadcast to any other part of the world. The B.B.C. now broadcasts in over 30 European languages, and nearly 50 languages in all—a complex job, when one remembers that so far as Britain is concerned the whole business of foreign radio propaganda has had to be improvised since 1938.

Probably the most useful section of Mr. Tangye Lean's book is a careful analysis of the radio campaign the Germans did during the Battle of France. They seem to have mixed truth and falsehood with extraordinary skill, giving strictly accurate news of military events but, at the same time, spreading wild rumours calculated to cause panic. The French radio hardly seems to have told the truth at any moment of the battle, and much of the time it simply gave no news at all. During the period of the phoney war the French had countered the German propaganda chiefly by means of jamming, a bad method, because it either does not work or, if it does work, gives the impression that something is being concealed. During the same period the Germans had sapped the morale of the French Army by clever radio programmes which gave the bored troops some light entertainment and, at the same time, stirred up Anglo-French jealousy and cashed in on the demagogic appeal of the Russo-German pact. When the French transmitter stations fell into their hands the Germans were ready with programmes of propaganda and music which they had prepared long beforehand—a detail of organisation which every invading army ought to keep in mind.

The Battle of France went so well for the Germans in a military sense that one may be inclined, when reading Mr. Tangye Lean's account, to overrate the part that radio played in their victory. A question Mr. Tangye Lean glances at but does not discuss at length is whether propaganda can ever achieve anything on its own, or whether it merely speeds up processes that are happening already. Probably the latter is the case, partly because the radio itself has had the unexpected effect of making war a more truthful business than it used to be. Except in a country like Japan, insulated by its remoteness and by the fact that the people have no shortwave sets, it is very difficult to conceal bad news, and if one is being reasonably truthful at home, it is difficult to tell very big lies to the enemy. Now and again a well-timed lie (examples are the Russian troops who passed through England in 1914, and the German Government's order to destroy all dogs in June, 1940) may produce a great effect, but in general propaganda cannot fight against the facts, though it can colour and distort them. It evidently does not pay, for any length of time, to say one thing and do another; the failure of the German New Order, not to take examples nearer home, has demonstrated this.

'Hitler can say that the Jews started the war, and if he survives that will become official history.'

to Noel Willmett, 18 May 1944, typewritten

10a Mortimer Crescent
London NW 6

Dear Mr Willmett,

Many thanks for your letter. You ask whether totalitarianism, leader-worship etc. are really on the up-grade and instance the fact that they are not apparently growing in this country and the USA.

I must say I believe, or fear, that taking the world as a whole these things are on the increase. Hitler, no doubt, will soon disappear, but only at the expense of strengthening (a) Stalin, (b) the Anglo-American millionaires and (c) all sorts of petty fuhrers of the type of de Gaulle. All the national movements everywhere, even those that originate in resistance to German domination, seem to take non-democratic forms, to group themselves round some superhuman fuhrer (Hitler, Stalin, Salazar, Franco, Gandhi, De Valera are all varying examples) and to adopt the theory that the end justifies the means. Everywhere the world movement seems to be in the direction of centralised economies which can be made to 'work' in an economic sense but which are not democratically organised and which tend to establish a caste system. With this go the horrors of emotional nationalism and a tendency to disbelieve in the existence of objective truth because all the facts have to fit in with the words and prophecies of some infallible fuhrer. Already history has in a sense ceased to exist, ie. there is no such thing as a history of our own times which could be universally accepted, and the exact sciences are endangered as soon as military necessity ceases to keep people up to the mark. Hitler can say that the Jews started the war, and if he survives that will become official history. He can't say that two and two are five, because for the purposes of, say, ballistics they have to make four. But if the sort of world that I am afraid of arrives, a world of two or three great superstates which are unable to conquer one another, two and two could become five if the fuhrer wished it. That, so far as I can see, is the direction in which we are actually moving, though, of course, the process is reversible.

[. . .]

Yours sincerely,
[signed] Geo. Orwell
George Orwell

'We are told that it is only people's objective actions that matter'

from 'As I Please', *Tribune*, 8 December 1944

FOR YEARS PAST I have been an industrious collector of pamphlets, and a fairly steady reader of political literature of all kinds. The thing that strikes me more and more—and it strikes a lot of other people, too—is the extraordinary viciousness and dishonesty of political controversy in our time. I don't mean merely that controversies are acrimonious. They ought to be that when they are on serious subjects. I mean that almost nobody seems to feel that an opponent deserves a fair hearing or that the objective truth matters so long as you can score a neat debating point. When I look through my collection of pamphlets—Conservative, Communist, Catholic, Trotskyist, Pacifist, Anarchist or what-have-you—it seems to me that almost all of them have the same mental atmosphere, though the points of emphasis vary. Nobody is searching for the truth, everybody is putting forward a 'case' with complete disregard for fairness or accuracy, and the most plainly obvious facts can be ignored by those who don't want to see them. The same propaganda tricks are to be found almost everywhere. It would take many pages of this paper merely to classify them, but here I draw attention to one very widespread controversial habit—disregard of an opponent's motives. The key-word here is 'objectively'.

We are told that it is only people's objective actions that matter, and their subjective feelings are of no importance. Thus, pacifists, by obstructing the war effort, are 'objectively' aiding the Nazis: and therefore the fact that they may be personally hostile to Fascism is irrelevant. I have been guilty of saying this myself more than once. The same argument is applied to Trotskyists. Trotskyists are often credited, at any rate by Communists, with being active and conscious agents of Hitler; but when you point out the many and obvious reasons why this is unlikely to be true, the 'objectively' line of talk is brought forward again. To criticise the Soviet Union helps Hitler: therefore 'Trotskyism is Fascism.' And when this has been established, the accusation of conscious treachery is usually repeated.

This is not only dishonest; it also carries a severe penalty with it. If you disregard people's motives, it becomes much harder to foresee their actions. For there are occasions when even the most misguided person can see the results of what he is doing. Here is a crude but quite possible illustration. A pacifist is working in some job which gives him access to important military information, and is approached by a German secret agent. In those circumstances his subjective feelings do make a difference. If he is subjectively pro-Nazi he will sell his country, and if he isn't, he won't. And situations essentially similar though less dramatic are constantly arising.

In my opinion a few pacifists are inwardly pro-Nazi, and extremist Left-wing parties will inevitably contain Fascist spies. The important thing is to discover which individuals are honest and which are not, and the usual blanket accusation merely makes this more difficult. The atmosphere of hatred in which controversy is conducted blinds people to considerations of this kind. To admit that an opponent might be both honest and intelligent is felt to be intolerable. It is more immediately satisfying to shout that he is a fool or a scoundrel, or both, than to find out what he is really like. It is this habit of mind, among other things, that has made political prediction in our time so remarkably unsuccessful.

'Nationalism is not to be confused with patriotism.'

from 'Notes on Nationalism', *Polemic*,
[October] 1945

BY 'NATIONALISM' I MEAN first of all the habit of assuming that human beings can be classified like insects and that whole blocks of millions or tens of millions of people can be confidently labelled 'good' or 'bad'. But secondly—and this is much more important—I mean the habit of identifying oneself with a single nation or other unit, placing it beyond good and evil and recognizing no other duty than that of advancing its interests. Nationalism is not to be confused with patriotism. Both words are normally used in so vague a way that any definition is liable to be challenged, but one must draw a distinction between them, since two different and even opposing ideas are involved. By 'patriotism' I mean devotion to a particular place and a particular way of life, which one believes to be the best in the world but has no wish to force upon other people. Patriotism is of its nature defensive, both militarily and culturally. Nationalism, on the other hand, is inseparable from the desire for power. The abiding purpose of every nationalist is to secure more power and more prestige, not for himself but for the nation or other unit in which he has chosen to sink his own individuality.

[. . .] Nationalism, in the extended sense in which I am using the word, includes such movements and tendencies as Communism, political Catholicism, Zionism, anti-Semitism, Trotskyism and Pacifism. It does not necessarily mean loyalty to a government or a country, still less to one's own country, and it is not even strictly necessary that the units in which it deals should actually exist. To name a few obvious examples, Jewry, Islam, Christendom, the Proletariat and the White Race are all of them the objects of passionate nationalistic feeling: but their existence can be seriously questioned, and there is no definition of any one of them that would be universally accepted.

[. . .] For those who feel deeply about contemporary politics, certain topics have become so infected by considerations of prestige that a genuinely rational approach to them is almost impossible. Out of the hundreds of examples that one might choose, take this question: Which of the three great allies, the U.S.S.R., Britain and the U.S.A., has contributed most to the defeat of Germany? In theory it should be possible to give a reasoned and perhaps even a conclusive answer to this question. In practice, however, the necessary calculations cannot be made, because anyone likely to bother his head about such a question would inevitably see it in terms of competitive prestige. He would therefore start by deciding in favour of Russia, Britain or America as the case might be, and only after this would begin searching for arguments that seemed to support his case. And there are whole strings of kindred questions to which you can only get an honest answer from someone who is indifferent to the whole subject involved, and whose opinion on it is probably worthless in any case. Hence, partly, the remarkable failure in our time of political and military prediction. It is curious to reflect that out of all the 'experts' of all the schools, there was not a single one who was able to foresee so likely an event as the Russo-German Pact of 1939.* And when the news of the Pact broke, the most wildly divergent explanations of it were given, and predictions were made which were falsified almost immediately, being based in nearly every case not on a study of probabilities but on a desire to make the U.S.S.R. seem good or bad, strong or weak. Political or military commentators, like

---

* A few writers of conservative tendency, such as Peter Drucker, foretold an agreement between Germany and Russia, but they expected an actual alliance or amalgamation which would be permanent. No Marxist or other left-wing writer, of whatever colour, came anywhere near foretelling the Pact.

astrologers, can survive almost any mistake, because their more devoted followers do not look to them for an appraisal of the facts but for the stimulation of nationalistic loyalties.* And æsthetic judgements, especially literary judgements, are often corrupted in the same way as political ones. It would be difficult for an Indian Nationalist to enjoy reading Kipling or for a Conservative to see merit in Mayakovsky, and there is always a temptation to claim that any book whose tendency one disagrees with must

---

* The military commentators of the popular press can mostly be classified as pro-Russian or anti-Russian, pro-blimp or anti-blimp. Such errors as believing the Maginot Line impregnable, or predicting that Russia would conquer Germany in three months, have failed to shake their reputation, because they are always saying what their own particular audience wanted to hear. The two military critics most favoured by the intelligentsia are Captain Liddell Hart and Major-General Fuller, the first of whom teaches that the defence is stronger than the attack, and the second that the attack is stronger than the defence. This contradiction has not prevented both of them from being accepted as authorities by the same public. The secret reason for their vogue in left-wing circles is that both of them are at odds with the War Office.

be a bad book from a *literary* point of view. People of strongly nationalistic outlook often perform this sleight of hand without being conscious of dishonesty.

'Indifference to reality.'

from 'Notes on Nationalism', *Polemic*, [October] 1945

Indifference to Reality. All nationalists have the power of not seeing resemblances between similar sets of facts. A British Tory will defend self-determination in Europe and oppose it in India with no feeling of inconsistency. Actions are held to be good or bad, not on their own merits but according to who does them, and there is almost no kind of outrage — torture, the use of hostages, forced labour, mass deportations, imprisonment without trial, forgery, assassination, the bombing of civilians — which does not change its moral colour when it is committed by 'our' side. The Liberal *News Chronicle* published, as an example of shocking barbarity, photographs of Russians hanged by the Germans, and then a year or two later published with warm approval almost exactly similar photographs of Germans hanged by the Russians.* It is the same with historical events. History is thought of largely in nationalist terms, and such things as the Inquisition, the tortures of the Star Chamber, the exploits of the English buccaneers (Sir Francis Drake, for instance, who was given to sinking Spanish prisoners alive), the Reign of Terror, the heroes of the Mutiny blowing hundreds of Indians from the guns, or Cromwell's soldiers slashing Irishwomen's faces with razors, become morally neutral or even meritorious when it is felt that they were done in 'the right' cause. If one looks back over the past quarter of a century, one finds that there was hardly a single year when atrocity stories were not being reported from some part of the world: and yet in not one single case were these atrocities—in Spain, Russia, China, Hun-

---

* The *News Chronicle* advised its readers to visit the news film at which the entire execution could be witnessed, with close-ups. The *Star* published with seeming approval photographs of nearly naked female collaborationists being baited by the Paris mob. These photographs had a marked resemblance to the Nazi photographs of Jews being baited by the Berlin mob.

gary, Mexico, Amritsar, Smyrna—believed in and disapproved of by the English intelligentsia as a whole. Whether such deeds were reprehensible, or even whether they happened, was always decided according to political predilection.

The nationalist not only does not disapprove of atrocities committed by his own side, but has a remarkable capacity for not even hearing about them. For quite six years the English admirers of Hitler contrived not to learn of the existence of Dachau and Buchenwald. And those who are loudest in denouncing the German concentration camps are often quite unaware, or only very dimly aware, that there are also concentration camps in Russia. Huge events like the Ukraine famine of 1933, involving the deaths of millions of people, have actually escaped the attention of the majority of English Russophiles. Many English people have heard almost nothing about the extermination of German and Polish Jews during the present war. Their own antisemitism has caused this vast crime to bounce off their consciousness. In nationalist thought there are facts which are both true and untrue, known and unknown. A known fact may be so unbearable that it is habitually pushed aside and not allowed to enter into logical processes, or on the other hand it may enter into every calculation and yet never be admitted as a fact, even in one's own mind.

Every nationalist is haunted by the belief that the past can be altered. He spends part of his time in a fantasy world in which things happen as they should—in which, for example, the Spanish Armada was a success or the Russian Revolution was crushed in 1918—and he will transfer fragments of this world to the history books whenever possible. Much of the propagandist writing of our time amounts to plain forgery. Material facts are suppressed, dates altered, quotations removed from their context and doctored so as to change their meaning. Events which, it is felt, ought not to have happened are left unmentioned and ultimately denied.* In 1927 Chiang Kai-Shek boiled

---

* An example is the Russo-German Pact, which is being effaced as quickly as possible from public memory. A Russian corre-

hundreds of Communists alive, and yet within ten years he had become one of the heroes of the Left. The realignment of world politics had brought him into the anti-Fascist camp, and so it was felt that the boiling of the Communists 'didn't count', or perhaps had not happened. The primary aim of propaganda is, of course, to influence contemporary opinion, but those who rewrite history do probably believe with part of their minds that they are actually thrusting facts into the past. When one considers the elaborate forgeries that have been committed in order to show that Trotsky did not play a valuable part in the Russian civil war, it is difficult to feel that the people responsible are merely lying. More probably they feel that their own version was what happened in the sight of God, and that one is justified in rearranging the records accordingly. Indifference to objective truth is encouraged by the sealing-off of one part of the world from another, which makes it

---

spondent informs me that mention of the pact is already being omitted from Russian books which table recent political events.

harder and harder to discover what is actually happening. There can often be a genuine doubt about the most enormous events. For example, it is impossible to calculate within millions, perhaps even tens of millions, the number of deaths caused by the present war. The calamities that are constantly being reported—battles, massacres, famines, revolutions—tend to inspire in the average person a feeling of unreality. One has no way of verifying the facts, one is not even fully certain that they have happened, and one is always presented with totally different interpretations from different sources. What were the rights and wrongs of the Warsaw rising of August 1944? Is it true about the German gas ovens in Poland? Who was really to blame for the Bengal famine? Probably the truth is discoverable, but the facts will be so dishonestly set forth in almost any newspaper that the ordinary reader can be forgiven either for swallowing lies or for failing to form an opinion. The general uncertainty as to what is really happening makes it easier to cling to lunatic beliefs. Since nothing is ever quite proved or disproved, the most unmistakable fact can be impudently denied. Moreover, although endlessly brooding on power, victory, defeat, revenge, the nationalist is often somewhat uninterested in what happens in the real world. What he wants is to *feel* that his own unit is getting the better of some other unit, and he can more easily do this by scoring off an adversary than by examining the facts to see whether they support him. All nationalist controversy is at the debating-society level. It is always entirely inconclusive, since each contestant invariably believes himself to have won the victory. Some nationalists are not far from schizophrenia, living quite happily amid dreams of power and conquest which have no connection with the physical world.

'Tactics, comrades, tactics!'

from *Animal Farm* (1945)

ON THE THIRD SUNDAY after Snowball's expulsion, the animals were somewhat surprised to hear Napoleon announce that the windmill was to be built after all. He did not give any reason for having changed his mind, but merely warned the animals that this extra task would mean very hard work; it might even be necessary to reduce their rations. [. . .]

That evening Squealer explained privately to the other animals that Napoleon had never in reality been opposed to the windmill. On the contrary, it was he who had advocated it in the beginning, and the plan which Snowball had drawn on the floor of the incubator shed had actually been stolen from among Napoleon's papers. The windmill was, in fact, Napoleon's own creation. Why, then, asked somebody, had he spoken so strongly against it? Here Squealer looked very sly. That, he said, was Comrade Napoleon's cunning. He had *seemed* to oppose the windmill, simply as a manoeuvre to get rid of Snowball, who was a dangerous character and a bad influence. Now that Snowball was out of the way the plan could go forward without his interference. This, said Squealer, was something called tactics. He repeated a number of times, 'Tactics, comrades, tactics!' skipping round and whisking his tail with a merry laugh. The animals were not certain what the word meant, but Squealer spoke so persuasively, and the three dogs who happened to be with him growled so threateningly, that they accepted his explanation without further questions.

'Doubtless it had been worse in the old days.'

from *Animal Farm* (1945)

THE WINTER WAS AS COLD as the last one had been, and food was even shorter. Once again all rations were reduced except those of the pigs and the dogs. A too-rigid equality in rations, Squealer explained, would have been contrary to the principles of Animalism. In any case he had no difficulty in proving to the other animals that they were *not* in reality short of food, whatever the appearances might be. For the time being, certainly, it had been found necessary to make a readjustment of rations (Squealer always spoke of it as a 'readjustment', never as a 'reduction'), but in comparison with the days of Jones the improvement was enormous. Reading out the figures in a shrill rapid voice, he proved to them in detail that they had more oats, more hay, more turnips than they had had in Jones's day, that they worked shorter hours, that their drinking water was of better quality, that they lived longer, that a larger proportion of their young ones survived infancy, and that they had more straw in their stalls and suffered less from fleas. The animals believed every word of it. Truth to tell, Jones and all he stood for had almost faded out of their memories. They knew that life nowadays was harsh and bare, that they were often hungry and often cold, and that they were usually working when they were not asleep. But doubtless it had been worse in the old days. They were glad to believe so. Besides, in those days they were slaves and now they were free, and that made all the difference, as Squealer did not fail to point out.

'Sugarcandy Mountain'

from *Animal Farm* (1945)

IN THE MIDDLE OF THE SUMMER Moses the raven suddenly reappeared on the farm, after an absence of several years. He was quite unchanged, still did no work, and talked in the same strain as ever about Sugarcandy Mountain [. . .] 'Up there, comrades,' he would say solemnly, pointing to the sky with his large beak – 'up there, just on the other side of that dark cloud you can see – there it lies, Sugarcandy Mountain, that happy country where we poor animals shall rest for ever from our labours!' He even claimed to have been there on one of his higher flights, and to have seen the everlasting fields of clover and the linseed cake and lump sugar growing on the hedges. Many of the animals believed him. Their lives now, they reasoned, were hungry and laborious; was it not right and just that a better world should exist somewhere else? A thing that was difficult to determine was the attitude of the pigs towards Moses. They all declared contemptuously that his stories about Sugarcandy Mountain were lies, and yet they allowed him to remain on the farm, not working, with an allowance of a gill of beer a day.

'I mentioned the reaction I had had from an important official in the Ministry of Information with regard to Animal Farm.'

from 'Publication of *Animal Farm:*
"The Freedom of the Press"',
London, 17 August 1945; New York, 26 August 1946

THIS BOOK WAS FIRST THOUGHT OF, so far as the central idea goes, in 1937, but was not written down until about the end of 1943. By the time when it came to be written it was obvious that there would be great difficulty in getting it published (in spite of the present book shortage which ensures that anything describable as a book will 'sell'), and in the event it was refused by four publishers. Only one of these had any ideological motive. Two had been publishing anti-Russian books for years, and the other had no noticeable political colour. One publisher actually started by accepting the book, but after making the preliminary arrangements he decided to consult the Ministry of Information, who appear to have warned him, or at any rate strongly advised him, against publishing it. Here is an extract from his letter:

> I mentioned the reaction I had had from an important official in the Ministry of Information with regard to *Animal Farm*. I must confess that this expression of opinion has given me seriously to think . . . I can see now that it might be regarded as something which it was highly ill-advised to publish at the present time. If the fable were addressed generally to dictators and dictatorships at large then publication would be all right, but the fable does follow, as I see now, so completely the progress of the Russian Soviets and their two dictators, that it can apply only to Russia, to the exclusion of the other dictatorships. Another thing: it would be less offensive if the predominant caste in the fable were not pigs.* I think the choice of pigs as the ruling

---

* It is not quite clear whether this suggested modification is Mr. . . .'s own idea, or originated with the Ministry of Information; but it seems to have the official ring about it.

caste will no doubt give offence to many people, and particularly to anyone who is a bit touchy, as undoubtedly the Russians are.

This kind of thing is not a good symptom. Obviously it is not desirable that a government department should have any power of censorship (except security censorship, which no one objects to in war time) over books which are not officially sponsored. But the chief danger to freedom of thought and speech at this moment is not the direct interference of the MOI or any official body. If publishers and editors exert themselves to keep certain topics out of print, it is not because they are frightened of prosecution but because they are frightened of public opinion. In this country intellectual cowardice is the worst enemy a writer or journalist has to face, and that fact does not seem to me to have had the discussion it deserves.

Any fairminded person with journalistic experience will admit that during this war official censorship has not been particularly irksome.

We have not been subjected to the kind of totalitarian 'co-ordination' that it might have been reasonable to expect. The press has some justified grievances, but on the whole the Government has behaved well and has been surprisingly tolerant of minority opinions. The sinister fact about literary censorship in England is that it is largely voluntary. Unpopular ideas can be silenced, and inconvenient facts kept dark, without the need for any official ban. Anyone who has lived long in a foreign country will know of instances of sensational items of news—things which on their own merits would get the big headlines—being kept right out of the British press, not because the Government intervened but because of a general tacit agreement that 'it wouldn't do' to mention that particular fact. So far as the daily newspapers go, this is easy to understand. The British press is extremely centralised, and most of it is owned by wealthy men who have every motive to be dishonest on certain important topics. But the same kind of veiled censorship also operates in books and periodicals, as well as in plays, films and radio. At any given moment there is an orthodoxy, a body of ideas which it is assumed that all right-thinking people will accept without question. It is not exactly forbidden to say this, that or the other, but it is 'not done' to say it, just as in mid–Victorian times it was 'not done' to mention trousers in the presence of a lady. Anyone who challenges the prevailing orthodoxy finds himself silenced with surprising effectiveness. A genuinely unfashionable opinion is almost never given a fair hearing, either in the popular press or in the highbrow periodicals. At this moment what is demanded by the prevailing orthodoxy is an uncritical admiration of Soviet Russia. Everyone knows this, nearly everyone acts on it. Any serious criticism of the Soviet régime, any disclosure of facts which the Soviet government would prefer to keep hidden, is next door to unprintable. And this nation-wide conspiracy to flatter our ally takes place, curiously enough, against a background of genuine intellectual tolerance. For though you are not allowed to criticise the Soviet government, at least you are reasonably free to criticise our own. Hardly anyone will print an attack on Stalin, but it is quite safe to attack Churchill, at any rate in books and periodicals. And throughout five years of war, during two or three of which we were fighting for national survival, countless books, pamphlets and articles advocating a compromise peace have been published without interference. More, they have been published without exciting much disapproval. So long as the prestige of the U.S.S.R. is not involved, the principle of free speech has been reasonably well upheld. There are other forbidden topics, and I shall mention some of them presently, but the prevailing attitude towards the U.S.S.R. is much the most serious symptom. It is, as it were, spontaneous, and is not due to the action of any pressure group.

'I suppose everyone's got a right to
their own opinion.'

from 'Publication of *Animal Farm*;
"The Freedom of the Press"'
London, 17 August 1945 New York, 26 August 1946

THE ISSUE INVOLVED HERE is quite a simple
one: Is every opinion, however unpopular—
however foolish, even—entitled to a hearing?
Put it in that form and nearly any English intellectual will feel that he ought to say 'Yes'. But
give it a concrete shape, and ask, 'How about
an attack on Stalin? Is that entitled to a hearing?', and the answer more often than not will
be 'No'. In that case the current orthodoxy
happens to be challenged, and so the principle
of free speech lapses. Now, when one demands
liberty of speech and of the press, one is not
demanding absolute liberty. There always must
be, or at any rate there always will be, some

THE TRUTH.

If the intellectual liberty which without a doubt has been one of the distinguishing marks of western civilisation means anything at all, it means that everyone shall have the right to say and to print what he believes to be the truth, provided only that it does not harm the rest of the community in some quite unmistakable way.

THE TRUTH.

If the intellectual liberty which without a doubt has been one of the distinguishing marks of western civilisation means anything at all, it means that everyone shall have the right to say and to print what he believes to be the truth, provided only that it does not harm the rest of the community in some quite unmistakable way.

THE TRUTH

degree of censorship, so long as organised societies endure. But freedom, as Rosa Luxembourg said, is 'freedom for the other fellow'. The same principle is contained in the famous words of Voltaire: 'I detest what you say; I will defend to the death your right to say it.' If the intellectual liberty which without a doubt has been one of the distinguishing marks of western civilisation means anything at all, it means that everyone shall have the right to say and to print what he believes to be the truth, provided only that it does not harm the rest of the community in some quite unmistakable way. Both capitalist democracy and the western versions of Socialism have till recently taken that principle for granted. Our Government, as I have already pointed out, still makes some show of respecting it. The ordinary people in the street—partly, perhaps, because they are not sufficiently interested in ideas to be intolerant about them—still vaguely hold that 'I suppose everyone's got a right to their own opinion.' It is only, or at any rate it is chiefly, the literary and scientific intelligentsia, the very people who ought to be the guardians of liberty, who are beginning to despise it, in theory as well as in practice.

IF
LIBERTY
MEANS ANYTHING
AT ALL IT MEANS THE
RIGHT TO TELL PEOPLE
WHAT THEY DO NOT
WANT TO HEAR.

'The enemies of intellectual liberty always try to present their case as a plea for discipline versus individualism.'

from 'The Prevention of Literature', *Polemic*, January 1946; *The Atlantic Monthly*, March 1947

IN OUR AGE, the idea of intellectual liberty is under attack from two directions. On the one side are its theoretical enemies, the apologists of totalitarianism, and on the other its immediate, practical enemies, monopoly and bureaucracy. Any writer or journalist who wants to retain his integrity finds himself thwarted by the general drift of society rather than by active persecution. The sort of things that are working against him are the concentration of the Press in the hands of a few rich men, the grip of monopoly on radio and the films, the unwillingness of the public to spend money on books, making it necessary for nearly every writer to earn part of his living by hackwork, the encroachment of official bodies like the M.O.I. and the British Council, which help the writer to keep alive but also waste his time and dictate his opinions, and the continuous war atmosphere of the past ten years, whose distorting effects no one has been able to escape. Everything in our age conspires to turn the writer, and every other kind of artist as well, into a minor official, working on themes handed to [him] from above and never telling what seems to him the whole of the truth. But in struggling against this fate he gets no help from his own side: that is, there is no large body of opinion which will assure him that he is in the right. In the past, at any rate throughout the Protestant centuries, the idea of rebellion and the idea of intellectual integrity were mixed up. A heretic — political, moral, religious, or aesthetic — was one who refused to outrage his own conscience. His outlook was summed up in the words of the Revivalist hymn:

> Dare to be a Daniel,
> Dare to stand alone;
> Dare to have a purpose firm,
> Dare to make it known.

To bring this hymn up to date one would have to add a 'Don't' at the beginning of each line. For it is the peculiarity of our age that the rebels against the existing order, at any rate the most numerous and characteristic of them, are also rebelling against the idea of individual integrity. 'Daring to stand alone' is ideologically criminal as well as practically dangerous. The independence of the writer and the artist is eaten away by vague economic forces, and at the same time it is undermined by those who should be its defenders. It is with the second process that I am concerned here.

Freedom of speech and of the Press are usually attacked by arguments which are not worth bothering about. Anyone who has experience in lecturing and debating knows them backwards. Here I am not trying to deal with the familiar claim that freedom is an illusion, or with the claim that there is more freedom in totalitarian countries than in democratic ones, but with the much more tenable and dangerous proposition that freedom is undesirable and that intellectual honesty is a form of anti-social selfishness. Although other aspects of the question are usually in the foreground, the controversy over freedom of speech and of the Press is at bottom a controversy over the desirability, or otherwise, of telling lies. What is really at issue is the right to report contemporary events truthfully, or as truthfully as is consistent with the ignorance, bias and self-deception from which every observer necessarily suffers. In saying this I may seem to be saying that straightforward 'reportage' is the only branch of literature that matters: but I will try to show later that at every literary level, and probably in every one of the arts, the same issue arises in more or less subtilised forms. Meanwhile, it is necessary to strip away the irrelevancies in which this controversy is usually wrapped up.

The enemies of intellectual liberty always try to present their case as a plea for discipline versus individualism. The issue truth-versus-untruth is as far as possible kept in the background. Although the point of emphasis may vary, the writer who refuses to sell his opinions is always branded as a mere egoist. He is accused, that is, either of wanting to shut himself up in an ivory tower, or of making an exhibitionist display of his own personality, or of resisting the inevitable current of history in an attempt to cling to unjustified privileges. The Catholic and the Communist are alike in assuming that an opponent cannot be both honest and intelligent. Each of them tacitly claims that 'the truth' has already been revealed, and that the heretic, if he is not simply a fool, is secretly aware of 'the truth' and merely resists it out of selfish motives. In Communist literature the attack on intellectual liberty is usually masked by oratory about 'petty-bourgeois individualism', 'the illusions of nineteenth-century liberalism', etc., and backed up by words of abuse such as 'romantic' and 'sentimental', which, since they do not have any agreed meaning, are difficult to answer. In this way the controversy is manœuvred away from its real issue. One can accept, and most enlightened people would accept, the Communist thesis that pure freedom will only exist in a classless society, and that one is most nearly free when one is working to bring about such a society. But slipped in with this is the quite unfounded claim that the Communist Party is itself aiming at the establishment of the classless society, and that in the U.S.S.R. this aim is actually on the way to being realised. If the first claim is allowed to entail the second, there is almost no assault on common sense and common decency that cannot be justified. But meanwhile, the real point has been dodged. Freedom of the intellect means the freedom to report what one has seen, heard, and felt, and not to be obliged to fabricate imaginary facts and feelings. The familiar tirades against 'escapism', 'individualism', 'romanticism' and so forth, are merely a forensic device, the aim of which is to make the perversion of history seem respectable.

Fifteen years ago, when one defended the freedom of the intellect, one had to defend it against Conservatives, against Catholics, and to some extent—for in England they were not of great importance—against Fascists. Today one has to defend it against Communists and 'fellow travellers'. One ought not to exaggerate the direct influence of the small English Communist Party, but there can be no question about the poisonous effect of the Russian *mythos* on English intellectual life. Because of it, known facts are suppressed and distorted to such an extent as to make it doubtful whether a true history of our times can ever be written. [. . .] The argument that to tell the truth would be 'inopportune' or would 'play into the hands of' somebody or other is felt to be unanswerable, and few people are bothered by the prospect that the lies which they condone will get out of the newspapers and into the history books.

The organised lying practised by totalitarian states is not, as is sometimes claimed, a temporary expedient of the same nature as military deception. It is something integral to totalitarianism, something that would still continue even if concentration camps and secret police forces had ceased to be necessary. Among intelligent Communists there is an underground legend to the effect that although the Russian government is obliged now to deal in lying propaganda, frame-up trials, and so forth, it is secretly recording the facts and will publish them at some future time. We can, I believe, be quite certain that this is not the case, because the mentality implied by such an action is that of a liberal historian who believes that the past cannot be altered and that a correct knowledge of history is valuable as a matter of course. From the totalitarian point of view history is something to be created rather than learned. A totalitarian state is in effect a theocracy, and its ruling caste, in order to keep its position, has to be thought of as infallible. But since, in practice, no one is infallible, it is frequently necessary to rearrange past events in order to show that this or that mistake was not made, or that this or that imaginary triumph actually happened. Then, again, every major change in policy demands a corresponding change of doctrine and a revaluation of prominent historical figures. This kind of thing happens everywhere, but clearly it is likelier to lead to outright falsification in societies where only one opinion is permissible at any given moment. Totalitarianism demands, in fact, the continuous alteration of the past, and in the long run probably demands a disbelief in the very existence of objective truth. The friends of totalitarianism in this country usually tend to argue that since absolute truth is not attainable, a big lie is no worse than a little lie. It is pointed out that all historical records are biased and inaccurate, or, on the other hand, that modern physics has proved that what seems to us the real world is an illusion, so that to believe in the evidence of one's senses is simply vulgar philistinism. A totalitarian society which succeeded in perpetuating itself would probably set up a schizophrenic system of thought, in which the laws of common sense held good in everyday life and in certain exact sciences, but could be disregarded by the politician, the historian, and the sociologist. Already there are countless people who would think it scandalous to falsify a scientific textbook, but would see nothing wrong in falsifying a historical fact. It is at the point where literature and politics cross that totalitarianism exerts its greatest pressure on the intellectual. The exact sciences are not, at this date, menaced to anything like the same extent. This difference partly accounts for the fact that in all countries it is easier for the scientists than for the writers to line up behind their respective governments.

'Political writing in our time consists almost entirely of prefabricated phrases bolted together like the pieces of a child's Meccano set.'

from 'The Prevention of Literature', *Polemic*, January 1946; *The Atlantic Monthly*, March 1947

POLITICAL WRITING IN OUR TIME consists almost entirely of prefabricated phrases bolted together like the pieces of a child's Meccano set. It is the unavoidable result of self-censorship. To write in plain, vigorous language one has to think fearlessly, and if one thinks fearlessly one cannot be politically orthodox. It might be otherwise in an 'age of faith', when the prevailing orthodoxy has been long established and is not taken too seriously. In that case it would be possible, or might be possible, for large areas of one's mind to remain unaffected by what one officially believed. Even so, it is worth noticing that prose literature almost disappeared during the only age of faith that Europe has ever enjoyed. Throughout the whole of the Middle

Ages there was almost no imaginative prose literature and very little in the way of historical writing: and the intellectual leaders of society expressed their most serious thoughts in a dead language which barely altered during a thousand years.

Totalitarianism, however, does not so much promise an age of faith as an age of schizophrenia. A society becomes totalitarian when its structure becomes flagrantly artificial: that is, when its ruling class has lost its function but succeeds in clinging to power by force or fraud. Such a society, no matter how long it persists, can never afford to become either tolerant or intellectually stable. It can never permit either the truthful recording of facts, or the emotional sincerity, that literary creation demands. But to be corrupted by totalitarianism one does not have to live in a totalitarian country. The mere prevalence of certain ideas can spread a poison that makes one subject after another impossible for literary purposes. Wherever there is an enforced orthodoxy—or even two orthodoxies, as often happens—good writing stops. This was well illustrated by the Spanish civil war. To many English intellectuals the war was a deeply moving experience, but not an experience about which they could write sincerely. There were only two things that you were allowed to say, and both of them were palpable lies: as a result, the war produced acres of print but almost nothing worth reading.

'The imagination, like certain wild animals, will not breed in captivity.'

from 'The Prevention of Literature', *Polemic*, January 1946; *The Atlantic Monthly*, March 1947

THE FACT IS THAT CERTAIN THEMES cannot be celebrated in words, and tyranny is one of them. No one ever wrote a good book in praise of the Inquisition. Poetry might survive in a totalitarian age, and certain arts or half-arts, such as architecture, might even find tyranny beneficial, but the prose writer would have no choice between silence and death. Prose literature as we know it is the product of rationalism, of the Protestant centuries, of the autonomous individual. And the destruction of intellectual liberty cripples the journalist, the sociological writer, the historian, the novelist, the critic, and the poet, in that order. In the future it is possible that a new kind of literature, not involving individual feeling or truthful observation, may arise, but no such thing is at present imaginable. It seems much likelier that if the liberal culture that we have lived in since the Renaissance actually comes to an end, the literary art will perish with it. [. . .] Not only is it doomed in any country which retains a totalitarian structure; but any writer who adopts the totalitarian outlook, who finds excuses for persecution and the falsification of reality, thereby destroys himself as a writer. There is no way out of this. No tirades against 'individualism' and 'the ivory tower', no pious platitudes to the effect that 'true individuality is only attained through identification with the community', can get over the fact that a bought mind is a spoiled mind. Unless spontaneity enters at some point or another, literary creation is impossible, and language itself becomes ossified. At some time in the future, if the human mind becomes something totally different from what it now is, we may learn to separate literary creation from intellectual honesty. At present we know only that the imagination, like certain wild animals,

The IMAGINATION, like
certain
wild animals,
will not breed
in captivity.

will not breed in captivity. Any writer or journalist who denies that fact—and nearly all the current praise of the Soviet Union contains or implies such a denial—is, in effect, demanding his own destruction.

'Political language has to consist largely of euphemism, question-begging and sheer cloudy vagueness.'

from 'Politics and the English Language',
Payments Book, 11 December 1945;
Horizon, April 1946

IN OUR TIME, POLITICAL SPEECH and writing are largely the defence of the indefensible. Things like the continuance of British rule in India, the Russian purges and deportations, the dropping of the atom bombs on Japan, can indeed be defended, but only by arguments which are too brutal for most people to face, and which do not square with the professed aims of political parties. Thus political language has to consist largely of euphemism, question-begging and sheer cloudy vagueness. Defenceless villages are bombarded from the air, the inhabitants driven out into the countryside, the cattle machine-gunned, the huts set on fire with incendiary bullets: this is called pacification. Millions of peasants are robbed of their farms and sent trudging along the roads with no more than they can carry: this is called transfer of population or rectification of frontiers. People are imprisoned for years without trial, or shot in the back of the neck or sent to die of scurvy in Arctic lumber camps: this is called elimination of unreliable elements. Such phraseology is needed if one wants to name things without calling up mental pictures of them. Consider for instance some comfortable English professor defending Russian totalitarianism. He cannot say outright, 'I believe in killing off your opponents when you can get good results by doing so'. Probably, therefore, he will say something like this:

'While freely conceding that the Soviet régime exhibits certain features which the humanitarian may be inclined to deplore, we must, I think, agree that a certain curtailment of the right to political opposition is an unavoidable concomitant of transitional periods, and that the rigours which the Russian people have been called upon to undergo have been amply justified in the sphere of concrete achievement.'

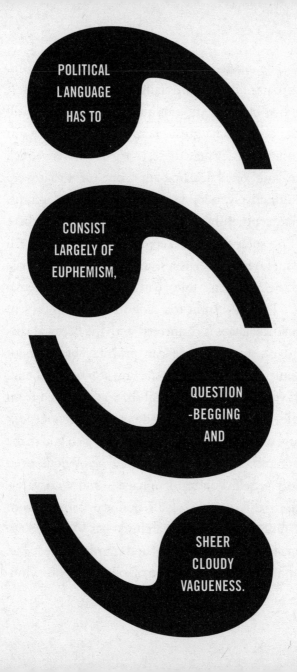

POLITICAL LANGUAGE HAS TO

CONSIST LARGELY OF EUPHEMISM,

QUESTION -BEGGING AND

SHEER CLOUDY VAGUENESS.

The inflated style is itself a kind of euphemism. A mass of Latin words falls upon the facts like soft snow, blurring the outlines and covering up all the details. The great enemy of clear language is insincerity. When there is a gap between one's real and one's declared aims, one turns as it were instinctively to long words and exhausted idioms, like a cuttlefish squirting out ink. In our age there is no such thing as 'keeping out of politics'. All issues are political issues, and politics itself is a mass of lies, evasions, folly, hatred and schizophrenia. [. . .] [O]ne ought to recognize that the present political chaos is connected with the decay of language, and that one can probably bring about some improvement by starting at the verbal end. If you simplify your English, you are freed from the worst follies of orthodoxy. You cannot speak any of the necessary dialects, and when you make a stupid remark its stupidity will be obvious, even to yourself. Political language—and with variations this is true of all political parties, from Conservatives to Anarchists—is designed to make lies sound truthful and murder respectable, and to give an appearance of solidity to pure wind.

TRUTH
LIES

Political language — and with variations this is
true of all political parties, from Conservatives to
Anarchists — is designed to make lies sound truthful
and murder respectable, and to give an
appearance of solidity to pure wind.

RESPECT
MURDER

'No book is genuinely free from political bias.'

from 'Why I Write' (1946)

PUTTING ASIDE THE NEED to earn a living, I think there are four great motives for writing, at any rate for writing prose. They exist in different degrees in every writer, and in any one writer the proportions will vary from time to time, according to the atmosphere in which he is living. They are:

(i) Sheer egoism. Desire to seem clever, to be talked about, to be remembered after death, to get your own back on grown-ups who snubbed you in childhood, etc., etc. It is humbug to pretend that this is not a motive, and a strong one. Writers share this characteristic with scientists, artists, politicians, lawyers, soldiers, successful businessmen—in short, with the whole top crust of humanity. The great mass of human beings are not acutely selfish. After the age of about thirty they abandon individual ambition—in many cases, indeed, they almost

abandon the sense of being individuals at all—
and live chiefly for others, or are simply
smothered under drudgery. But there is also the
minority of gifted, wilful people who are
determined to live their own lives to the end,
and writers belong in this class. Serious writers,
I should say, are on the whole more vain and
self-centred than journalists, though less interested in money.

(ii) Aesthetic enthusiasm. Perception of beauty
in the external world, or, on the other hand, in
words and their right arrangement. Pleasure in
the impact of one sound on another, in the firm-
ness of good prose or the rhythm of a good story.
Desire to share an experience which one feels is
valuable and ought not to be missed. The aesthetic motive is very feeble in a lot of writers, but
even a pamphleteer or a writer of textbooks will
have pet words and phrases which appeal to him
for non-utilitarian reasons; or he may feel
strongly about typography, width of margins,
etc. Above the level of a railway guide, no book
is quite free from æsthetic considerations.

(iii) Historical impulse. Desire to see things

as they are, to find out true facts and store them up for the use of posterity.

(iv) Political purpose—using the word 'political' in the widest possible sense. Desire to push the world in a certain direction, to alter other people's idea of the kind of society that they should strive after. Once again, no book is genuinely free from political bias. The opinion that art should have nothing to do with politics is itself a political attitude.

[. . .] What I have most wanted to do throughout the past ten years is to make political writing into an art. My starting point is always a feeling of partisanship, a sense of injustice. When I sit down to write a book, I do not say to myself, 'I am going to produce a work of art'. I write it because there is some lie that I want to expose, some fact to which I want to draw attention, and my initial concern is to get a hearing. But I could not do the work of writing a book, or even a long magazine article, if it were not also an aesthetic experience. Anyone who cares to examine my work will see that even when it is downright propaganda it contains much that a full-time politician would consider irrelevant. I am not able, and I do not want, completely to abandon the world-view that I acquired in childhood. So long as I remain alive and well I shall continue to feel strongly about prose style, to love the surface of the earth, and to take a pleasure in solid objects and scraps of useless information. It is no use trying to suppress that side of myself. The job is to reconcile my ingrained likes and dislikes with the essentially public, non-individual activities that this age forces on all of us.

It is not easy. It raises problems of construction and of language, and it raises in a new way the problem of truthfulness. Let me give just one example of the cruder kind of difficulty that arises. My book about the Spanish Civil War, *Homage to Catalonia*, is, of course, a frankly political book, but in the main it is written with a certain detachment and regard for form. I did try very hard in it to tell the whole truth without violating my literary instincts. But among other things it contains a long chapter, full of newspaper quotations and

FROM POLITICAL BIAS. **No BOOK** *IS GENUINELY* **FREE**

the like, defending the Trotskyists who were accused of plotting with Franco. Clearly such a chapter, which after a year or two would lose its interest for any ordinary reader, must ruin the book. A critic whom I respect read me a lecture about it. 'Why did you put in all that stuff?' he said. 'You've turned what might have been a good book into journalism.' What he said was true, but I could not have done otherwise. I happened to know, what very few people in England had been allowed to know, that innocent men were being falsely accused. If I had not been angry about that I should never have written the book.

In one form or another this problem comes up again. The problem of language is subtler and would take too long to discuss. I will only say that of late years I have tried to write less picturesquely and more exactly. In any case I find that by the time you have perfected any style of writing, you have always outgrown it. *Animal Farm* was the first book in which I tried, with full consciousness of what I was doing, to fuse political purpose and artistic purpose into one whole. I have not written a novel for seven years, but I hope to write another fairly soon. It is bound to be a failure, every book is a failure, but I do know with some clarity what kind of book I want to write.

Looking back through the last page or two, I see that I have made it appear as though my motives in writing were wholly public-spirited. I don't want to leave that as the final impression. All writers are vain, selfish and lazy, and at the very bottom of their motives there lies a mystery. Writing a book is a horrible, exhausting struggle, like a long bout of some painful illness. One would never undertake such a thing if one were not driven on by some demon whom one can neither resist nor understand. For all one knows that demon is simply the same instinct that makes a baby squall for attention. And yet it is also true that one can write nothing readable unless one constantly struggles to efface one's own personality. Good prose is like a window pane. I cannot say with certainty which of my motives are the strongest, but I know which of them deserve to be followed. And looking back through my work, I see that it is invariably where I lacked a political purpose that I wrote lifeless books and was betrayed into purple passages, sentences without meaning, decorative adjectives and humbug generally.

'A nation gets the newspapers it deserves.'

from 'As I Please', *Tribune*, 22 November 1946

IN CURRENT DISCUSSIONS of the Royal Commission that is to inquire into the Press, the talk is always of the debasing influence exerted by owners and advertisers. It is not said often enough that a nation gets the newspapers it deserves. Admittedly, this is not the whole of the truth. When the bulk of the Press is owned by a handful of people, one has not much choice, and the fact that during the war the newspapers temporarily became more intelligent, without losing circulation, suggests that the public taste is not quite so bad as it seems. Still, our newspapers are not all alike; some of them are more intelligent than others, and some are more popular than others. And when you study the relationship between intelligence and popularity, what do you find?

Below I list in two columns our nine leading national daily papers. In the first column these are ranged in order of intelligence, so far as I am able to judge it: in the other they are ranged in order of popularity, as measured by circulation. By intelligence I do not mean agreement with my own opinions. I mean a readiness to present news objectively, to give prominence to the things that really matter, to discuss serious questions even when they are dull, and to advocate policies which are at least coherent and intelligible. As to the circulation, I may have misplaced one or two papers, as I have no recent figures, but my list will not be far out. Here are the two lists:

INTELLIGENCE	POPULARITY
1. *Manchester Guardian.*	1. *Express.*
2. *Times.*	2. *Herald.*
3. *News Chronicle.*	3. *Mirror.*
4. *Telegraph.*	4. *News Chronicle.*
5. *Herald.*	5. *Mail.*
6. *Mail.*	6. *Graphic.*
7. *Mirror.*	7. *Telegraph.*
8. *Express.*	8. *Times.*
9. *Graphic.*	9. *Manchester Guardian.*

It will be seen that the second list is very nearly—not quite, for life is never so neat as that—the first turned upside down. And even if I have not ranged these papers in quite the right order, the general relationship holds good. The paper that has the best reputation for truthfulness, the *Manchester Guardian*, is the one that is not read even by those who admire it. People complain that it is 'so dull'. On the other hand countless people read the *Daily*—while saying frankly that they 'don't believe a word of it'.

In these circumstances it is difficult to foresee a radical change, even if the special kind of pressure exerted by owners and advertisers is removed. What matters is that in England we do possess juridical liberty of the Press, which makes it possible to utter one's true opinions fearlessly in papers of comparatively small circulation. It is vitally important to hang on to that. But no Royal Commission can make the big-circulation Press much better than it is, however much it manipulates the methods of control. We shall have a serious and truthful popular Press when public opinion actively demands it. Till then, if the news is not distorted by businessmen it will be distorted by bureaucrats, who are only one degree better.

'WAR IS PEACE'

from *Nineteen Eighty-Four* (1949)

BEHIND WINSTON'S BACK THE VOICE from the telescreen was still babbling away about pig-iron and the overfulfilment of the Ninth Three-Year Plan. The telescreen received and transmitted simultaneously. Any sound that Winston made, above the level of a very low whisper, would be picked up by it; moreover, so long as he remained within the field of vision which the metal plaque commanded, he could be seen as well as heard. There was of course no way of knowing whether you were being watched at any given moment. How often, or on what system, the Thought Police plugged in on any individual wire was guesswork. It was even conceivable that they watched everybody all the time. But at any rate they could plug in your wire whenever they wanted to. You had to live — did live, from habit that became instinct — in the assumption that every sound you made was overheard, and, except in darkness, every movement scrutinised.

Winston kept his back turned to the telescreen. It was safer; though, as he well knew, even a back can be revealing. A kilometre away the Ministry of Truth, his place of work, towered vast and white above the grimy landscape. This, he thought with a sort of vague distaste—this was London, chief city of Airstrip One, itself the third most populous of the provinces of Oceania. He tried to squeeze out some childhood memory that should tell him whether London had always been quite like this. Were there always these vistas of rotting nineteenth-century houses, their sides shored up with baulks of timber, their windows patched with cardboard and their roofs with corrugated iron, their crazy garden walls sagging in all directions? And the bombed sites where the plaster dust swirled in the air and the willowherb straggled over the heaps of rubble; and the places where the bombs had cleared a larger patch and there had sprung up sordid colonies of wooden dwellings like chicken-houses? But it was no use, he could not remember: nothing remained of his childhood except a series of bright-lit tableaux, occurring against no background and mostly unintelligible.

The Ministry of Truth—Minitrue, in Newspeak—was startlingly different from any other object in sight. It was an enormous pyramidal structure of glittering white concrete, soaring up, terrace after terrace, three hundred metres into the air. From where Winston stood it was just possible to read, picked out on its white face in elegant lettering, the three slogans of the Party:

WAR IS PEACE
FREEDOM IS SLAVERY
IGNORANCE IS STRENGTH.

[. . .] The thing that he was about to do was to open a diary. This was not illegal (nothing was illegal, since there were no longer any laws), but if detected it was reasonably certain that it would be punished by death, or at least by twenty-five years in a forced-labour camp. Winston fitted a nib into the penholder and sucked it to get the grease off. The pen was an archaic instrument, seldom used even for signatures, and he had procured one, furtively and with some difficulty, simply because of a feeling that the beautiful creamy paper deserved to be written on with a real nib instead of being scratched with an ink-pencil. Actually he was not used to writing by hand. Apart from very short notes, it was usual to dictate everything into the speakwrite, which was of course impossible for his present purpose. He dipped the pen into the ink and then faltered for just a second. A tremor had gone through his bowels. To mark the paper was the decisive act. In small clumsy letters he wrote:

April 4th, 1984.

He sat back. A sense of complete helplessness had descended upon him. To begin with he did not know with any certainty that this was 1984. It must be round about that date, since he was fairly sure that his age was thirty-nine, and he believed that he had been born in 1944 or 1945; but it was never possible nowadays to pin down any date within a year or two.

For whom, it suddenly occurred to him to wonder, was he writing this diary? For the future, for the unborn. His mind hovered for a moment round the doubtful date on the page, and then fetched up with a bump against the Newspeak word *doublethink*. For the first time the magnitude of what he had undertaken came home to him. How could you communicate with the future? It was of its nature impossible. Either the future would resemble the present, in which case it would not listen to him: or it would be different from it, and his predicament would be meaningless.

'When there were no external records that you could refer to, even the outline of your own life lost its sharpness.'

from *Nineteen Eighty-Four* (1949)

THE TELESCREEN WAS GIVING FORTH an ear-splitting whistle which continued on the same note for thirty seconds. It was nought seven fifteen, getting-up time for office workers. Winston wrenched his body out of bed—naked, for a member of the Outer Party received only three thousand clothing coupons annually, and a suit of pyjamas was six hundred—and seized a dingy singlet and a pair of shorts that were lying across a chair. The Physical Jerks would begin in three minutes. The next moment he was doubled up by a violent coughing fit which nearly always attacked him soon after waking up. It emptied his lungs so completely that he could only begin breathing again by lying on his back and taking a series of deep gasps. His veins had swelled with the effort of the cough, and the varicose ulcer had started itching.

'Thirty to forty group!' yapped a piercing female voice. 'Thirty to forty group! Take your places, please. Thirties to forties!'

Winston sprang to attention in front of the telescreen, upon which the image of a youngish woman, scrawny but muscular, dressed in tunic and gym-shoes, had already appeared.

'Arms bending and stretching!' she rapped out. 'Take your time by me. *One*, two, three, four! *One*, two, three, four! Come on, comrades, put a bit of life into it! *One*, two, three, four! *One*, two, three, four! . . .'

The pain of the coughing fit had not quite driven out of Winston's mind the impression made by his dream, and the rhythmic movements of the exercise restored it somewhat. As he mechanically shot his arms back and forth, wearing on his face the look of grim enjoyment which was considered proper during the Physical Jerks, he was struggling to think his way backward into the dim period of his early childhood. It was extraordinarily difficult.

Beyond the late 'fifties everything faded. When there were no external records that you could refer to, even the outline of your own life lost its sharpness. You remembered huge events which had quite probably not happened, you remembered the detail of incidents without being able to recapture their atmosphere, and there were long blank periods to which you could assign nothing. Everything had been different then. Even the names of countries, and their shapes on the map, had been different. Airstrip One, for instance, had not been so called in those days: it had been called England or Britain, though London, he felt fairly certain, had always been called London.

[. . .] For several months during his childhood there had been confused street fighting in London itself, some of which he remembered vividly. But to trace out the history of the whole period, to say who was fighting whom at any given moment, would have been utterly impossible, since no written record, and no spoken word, ever made mention of any other alignment than the existing one. At this moment, for example, in 1984 (if it was 1984), Oceania was at war with Eurasia and in alliance with Eastasia. In no public or private utterance was it ever admitted that the three powers had at any time been grouped along different lines. Actually, as Winston well knew, it was only four years since Oceania had been at war with Eastasia and in alliance with Eurasia. But that was merely a piece of furtive knowledge which he happened to possess because his memory was not satisfactorily under control. Officially the change of partners had never happened. Oceania was at war with Eurasia: therefore Oceania had always been at war with Eurasia. The enemy of the moment always represented absolute evil, and it followed that any past or future agreement with him was impossible.

The frightening thing, he reflected for the ten thousandth time as he forced his shoulders painfully backward (with hands on hips, they were gyrating their bodies from the waist, an exercise that was supposed to be good for the back muscles)—the frightening thing was that it might all be true. If the Party could thrust its

'Who controls

THE PAST,'

ran the Party slogan,

'controls

THE FUTURE:

who controls

THE PRESENT

controls

THE PAST.'

hand into the past and say of this or that event, *it never happened*—that, surely, was more terrifying than mere torture and death?

The Party said that Oceania had never been in alliance with Eurasia. He, Winston Smith, knew that Oceania had been in alliance with Eurasia as short a time as four years ago. But where did that knowledge exist? Only in his own consciousness, which in any case must soon be annihilated. And if all others accepted the lie which the Party imposed—if all records told the same tale—then the lie passed into history and became truth. 'Who controls the past,' ran the Party slogan, 'controls the future: who controls the present controls the past.' And yet the past, though of its nature alterable, never had been altered. Whatever was true now was true from everlasting to everlasting. It was quite simple. All that was needed was an unending series of victories over your own memory. 'Reality control', they called it: in Newspeak, 'doublethink'.

[. . .] Winston sank his arms to his sides and slowly refilled his lungs with air. His mind slid away into the labyrinthine world of doublethink. To know and not to know, to be conscious of complete truthfulness while telling carefully-constructed lies, to hold simultaneously two opinions which cancelled out, knowing them to be contradictory and believing in both of them; to use logic against logic, to repudiate morality while laying claim to it, to believe that democracy was impossible and that the Party was the guardian of democracy; to forget whatever it was necessary to forget, then to draw it back into memory again at the moment when it was needed, and then promptly to forget it again: and above all, to apply the same process to the process itself. That was the ultimate subtlety: consciously to induce unconsciousness, and then, once again, to become unconscious of the act of hypnosis you had just performed. Even to understand the word 'doublethink' involved the use of doublethink. [. . .] The past, he reflected, had not merely been altered, it had been actually destroyed. For how could you establish even the most obvious fact when there existed no record outside your own memory? He tried to remember in what year he had first heard mention of Big Brother. He thought it must have been at some time in the 'sixties, but it was impossible to be certain. In the Party histories, of course, Big Brother figured as the leader and guardian of the Revolution since its very earliest days. His exploits had been gradually pushed backwards in time until already they extended into the fabulous world of the 'forties and the 'thirties, when the capitalists in their strange cylindrical hats still rode through the streets of London in great gleaming motor-cars or horse carriages with glass sides. There was no knowing how much of this legend was true and how much invented. Winston could not even remember at what date the Party itself had come into existence. He did not believe he had ever heard the word Ingsoc before 1960, but it was possible that in its Oldspeak form — 'English Socialism', that is to say — it had been current earlier. Everything melted into mist. Sometimes indeed, you could put your finger on a definite lie. It was not true, for example, as was claimed in the Party history books, that the Party had invented aeroplanes. He remembered aeroplanes since his earliest childhood. But you could prove nothing.

'It's a beautiful thing, the destruction of words.'

from *Nineteen Eighty-Four* (1949)

IN THE LOW-CEILINGED CANTEEN, deep under ground, the lunch queue jerked slowly forward. The room was already very full and deafeningly noisy. From the grille at the counter the steam of stew came pouring forth, with a sour metallic smell which did not quite overcome the fumes of Victory Gin. On the far side of the room there was a small bar, a mere hole in the wall, where gin could be bought at ten cents the large nip.

'Just the man I was looking for,' said a voice at Winston's back.

He turned round. It was his friend Syme, who worked in the Research Department. Perhaps 'friend' was not exactly the right word. You did not have friends nowadays, you had comrades: but there were some comrades whose society was pleasanter than that of others. Syme was a philologist, a specialist in

Newspeak. Indeed, he was one of the enormous team of experts now engaged in compiling the Eleventh Edition of the Newspeak Dictionary. [. . .]

'How is the Dictionary getting on?' said Winston, raising his voice to overcome the noise.

'Slowly,' said Syme. 'I'm on the adjectives. It's fascinating.'

He had brightened up immediately at the mention of Newspeak. He pushed his pannikin aside, took up his hunk of bread in one delicate hand and his cheese in the other, and leaned across the table so as to be able to speak without shouting.

'The Eleventh Edition is the definitive edition,' he said. 'We're getting the language into its final shape—the shape it's going to have when nobody speaks anything else. When we've finished with it, people like you will have to learn it all over again. You think, I dare say, that our chief job is inventing new words. But not a bit of it! We're destroying words—scores of them, hundreds of them, every day. We're cutting the language down to the bone. The Eleventh Edition won't contain a single word that will become obsolete before the year 2050.'

He bit hungrily into his bread and swallowed a couple of mouthfuls, then continued speaking, with a sort of pedant's passion. His thin dark face had become animated, his eyes had lost their mocking expression and grown almost dreamy.

'It's a beautiful thing, the destruction of words. Of course the great wastage is in the verbs and adjectives, but there are hundreds of nouns that can be got rid of as well. It isn't only the synonyms; there are also the antonyms. After all, what justification is there for a word which is simply the opposite of some other word? A word contains its opposite in itself. Take "good", for instance. If you have a word like "good", what need is there for a word like "bad"? "Ungood" will do just as well— better, because it's an exact opposite, which the other is not. Or again, if you want a stronger version of "good", what sense is there in having a whole string of vague useless words like "excellent" and and all the rest of them? "Plusgood" covers the meaning; or "double-plusgood" if you want something stronger still. Of course we use those forms already, but in the final version of Newspeak there'll be nothing else. In the end the whole notion of goodness and badness will be covered by only six words—in reality, only one word. Don't you see the beauty of that, Winston? It was B.B.'s idea originally, of course,' he added as an afterthought.

A sort of vapid eagerness flitted across Winston's face at the mention of Big Brother. Nevertheless Syme immediately detected a certain lack of enthusiasm.

'You haven't a real appreciation of Newspeak, Winston,' he said almost sadly. 'Even when you write it you're still thinking in Oldspeak. I've read some of those pieces that you write in the *Times* occasionally. They're good enough, but they're translations. In your heart you'd prefer to stick to Oldspeak, with all its vagueness and its useless shades of meaning.

You don't grasp the beauty of the destruction of words. Do you know that Newspeak is the only language in the world whose vocabulary gets smaller every year?'

Winston did know that, of course. He smiled, sympathetically he hoped, not trusting himself to speak. Syme bit off another fragment of the dark-coloured bread, chewed it briefly, and went on:

'Don't you see that the whole aim of Newspeak is to narrow the range of thought? In the end we shall make thoughtcrime literally impossible, because there will be no words in which to express it. Every concept that can ever be needed will be expressed by exactly one word, with its meaning rigidly defined and all its subsidiary meanings rubbed out and forgotten. Already, in the Eleventh Edition, we're not far from that point. But the process will still be continuing long after you and I are dead. Every year fewer and fewer words, and the range of consciousness always a little smaller. Even now, of course, there's no reason or excuse for committing thought crime. It's merely a question of self-discipline, reality-control. But in the end there won't be any need even for that. The Revolution will be complete when the language is perfect. Newspeak is Ingsoc and Ingsoc is Newspeak,' he added with a sort of mystical satisfaction. 'Has it ever occurred to you, Winston, that by the year 2050, at the very latest, not a single human being will be alive who could understand such a conversation as we are having now?'

'Except—' began Winston doubtfully, and then stopped.

It had been on the tip of his tongue to say 'Except the proles,' but he checked himself, not feeling fully certain that this remark was not in some way unorthodox. Syme, however, had divined what he was about to say.

'The proles are not human beings,' he said carelessly. 'By 2050—earlier, probably—all real knowledge of Oldspeak will have disappeared. The whole literature of the past will have been destroyed. Chaucer, Shakespeare, Milton, Byron—they'll exist only in Newspeak versions, not merely changed into something different, but actually changed into something contradictory of what they used to be. Even the literature of the Party will change. Even the slogans will change. How could you have a slogan like "freedom is slavery" when the concept of freedom has been abolished? The whole climate of thought will be different. In fact there will *be* no thought, as we understand it now. Orthodoxy means not thinking—not needing to think. Orthodoxy is unconsciousness.'

One of these days, thought Winston with sudden deep conviction, Syme will be vaporized. He is too intelligent. He sees too clearly and speaks too plainly. The Party does not like such people. One day he will disappear. It is written in his face.

'*Crimestop* means the faculty of stopping short, as though by instinct, at the threshold of any dangerous thought.'

from *Nineteen Eighty-Four* (1949)

A PARTY MEMBER IS REQUIRED to have not only the right opinions, but the right instincts. Many of the beliefs and attitudes demanded of him are never plainly stated, and could not be stated without laying bare the contradictions inherent in Ingsoc. If he is a person naturally orthodox (in Newspeak a *goodthinker*), he will in all circumstances know, without taking thought, what is the true belief or the desirable emotion. But in any case an elaborate mental training, undergone in childhood and grouping itself round the Newspeak words *crimestop*, *blackwhite* and *doublethink*, makes him unwilling and unable to think too deeply on any subject whatever.

A Party member is expected to have no private emotions and no respites from enthusiasm.

He is supposed to live in a continuous frenzy of hatred of foreign enemies and internal traitors, triumph over victories, and self-abasement before the power and wisdom of the Party. The discontents produced by his bare, unsatisfying life are deliberately turned outwards and dissipated by such devices as the Two Minutes Hate, and the speculations which might possibly induce a sceptical or rebellious attitude are killed in advance by his early-acquired inner discipline. The first and simplest stage in the discipline, which can be taught even to young children, is called, in Newspeak, *crimestop*. *Crimestop* means the faculty of stopping short, as though by instinct, at the threshold of any dangerous thought. It includes the power of not grasping analogies, of failing to perceive logical errors, of misunderstanding the simplest arguments if they are inimical to Ingsoc, and of being bored or repelled by any train of thought which is capable of leading in a heretical direction. *Crimestop*, in short, means protective stupidity. But stupidity is not enough. On the contrary, orthodoxy in the full sense demands a control over one's own

CRIME STOP

MEANS THE FACULTY OF STOPPING SHORT, AS THOUGH BY INSTINCT, AT THE THRESHOLD OF ANY DANGEROUS THOUGHT.

mental processes as complete as that of a contortionist over his body. Oceanic society rests ultimately on the belief that Big Brother is omnipotent and that the Party is infallible. But since in reality Big Brother is not omnipotent and the Party is not infallible, there is need for an unwearying, moment-to-moment flexibility in the treatment of facts. The key-word here is *blackwhite*. Like so many Newspeak words, this word has two mutually contradictory meanings. Applied to an opponent, it means the habit of impudently claiming that black is white, in contradiction of the plain facts. Applied to a Party member, it means a loyal willingness to say that black is white when Party discipline demands this. But it means also the ability to *believe* that black is white, and more, to *know* that black is white, and to forget that one has ever believed the contrary.

'Is it your opinion, Winston, that the past has real existence?'

from *Nineteen Eighty-Four* (1949)

HE DID NOT REMEMBER any ending to his interrogation. There was a period of blackness and then the cell, or room, in which he now was had gradually materialised round him. He was almost flat on his back, and unable to move. His body was held down at every essential point. Even the back of his head was gripped in some manner. O'Brien was looking down at him gravely and rather sadly. His face, seen from below, looked coarse and worn, with pouches under the eyes and tired lines from nose to chin. He was older than Winston had thought him; he was perhaps forty-eight or fifty. Under his hand there was a dial with a lever on top and figures running round the face.

'I told you,' said O'Brien, 'that if we met again it would be here.'

'Yes,' said Winston.

Without any warning except a slight movement of O'Brien's hand, a wave of pain flooded
his body. It was a frightening pain, because
he could not see what was happening, and he
had the feeling that some mortal injury was being done to him. He did not know whether the
thing was really happening, or whether the effect
was electrically produced; but his body was being wrenched out of shape, the joints were being slowly torn apart. Although the pain had
brought the sweat out on his forehead, the
worst of all was the fear that his backbone was
about to snap. He set his teeth and breathed
hard through his nose, trying to keep silent as
long as possible.

'You are afraid,' said O'Brien, watching his
face, 'that in another moment something is
going to break. Your especial fear is that it will
be your backbone. You have a vivid mental picture of the vertebrae snapping apart and the
spinal fluid dripping out of them. That is what
you are thinking, is it not, Winston?'

Winston did not answer. O'Brien drew back

the lever on the dial. The wave of pain receded almost as quickly as it had come.

'That was forty,' said O'Brien. 'You can see that the numbers on this dial run up to a hundred. Will you please remember, throughout our conversation, that I have it in my power to inflict pain on you at any moment and to whatever degree I choose. If you tell me any lies, or attempt to prevaricate in any way, or even fall below your usual level of intelligence, you will cry out with pain, instantly. Do you understand that?'

'Yes,' said Winston.'

[. . .] O'Brien was looking down at him speculatively. More than ever he had the air of a teacher taking pains with a wayward but promising child.

'There is a Party slogan dealing with the control of the past,' he said. 'Repeat it, if you please.'

' "Who controls the past controls the future: who controls the present controls the past," ' repeated Winston obediently.

' "Who controls the present controls the past," ' said O'Brien, nodding his head with slow approval. 'Is it your opinion, Winston, that the past has real existence?'

Again the feeling of helplessness descended upon Winston. His eyes flitted towards the dial. He not only did not know whether 'yes' or 'no' was the answer that would save him from pain; he did not even know which answer he believed to be the true one.

O'Brien smiled faintly. 'You are no metaphysician, Winston,' he said. 'Until this moment you had never considered what is meant by existence. I will put it more precisely. Does the past exist concretely, in space? Is there somewhere or other a place, a world of solid objects, where the past is still happening?'

'No.'

'Then where does the past exist, if at all?'

'In records. It is written down.'

'In records. And – ?'

'In the mind. In human memories.'

'In memory. Very well, then. We, the Party, control all records, and we control all memories. Then we control the past, do we not?'

'But how can you stop people remembering

things?' cried Winston, again momentarily forgetting the dial. 'It is involuntary. It is outside oneself. How can you control memory? You have not controlled mine!'

O'Brien's manner grew stern again. He laid his hand on the dial.

'On the contrary,' he said, '*you* have not controlled it. That is what has brought you here. You are here because you have failed in humility, in self-discipline. You would not make the act of submission which is the price of sanity. You preferred to be a lunatic, a minority of one. Only the disciplined mind can see reality, Winston. You believe that reality is something objective, external, existing in its own right. You also believe that the nature of reality is self-evident. When you delude yourself into thinking that you see something, you assume that everyone else sees the same thing as you. But I tell you, Winston, that reality is not external. Reality exists in the human mind, and nowhere else. Not in the individual mind, which can make mistakes, and in any case soon perishes: only in the mind of the Party, which is collective and immortal. Whatever the Party holds to be truth, *is* truth. It is impossible to see reality except by looking through the eyes of the Party. That is the fact that you have got to re-learn, Winston. It needs an act of self-destruction, an effort of the will. You must humble yourself before you can become sane.'

He paused for a few moments, as though to allow what he had been saying to sink in.

'Do you remember,' he went on, 'writing in your diary, "Freedom is the freedom to say that two plus two make four"?'

'Yes,' said Winston.

O'Brien held up his left hand, its back towards Winston, with the thumb hidden and the four fingers extended.

'How many fingers am I holding up, Winston?'

'Four.'

'And if the Party says that it is not four but five – then how many?'

'Four.'

The word ended in a gasp of pain. The needle of the dial had shot up to fifty-five. The sweat

FREEDOM

IS THE FREEDOM TO SAY

$$\frac{\text{that two} \quad \text{plus two}}{\text{make four.}}$$

had sprung out all over Winston's body. The air tore into his lungs and issued again in deep groans which even by clenching his teeth he could not stop. O'Brien watched him, the four fingers still extended. He drew back the lever. This time the pain was only slightly eased.

'How many fingers, Winston?'

'Four.'

The needle went up to sixty.

'How many fingers, Winston?'

'Four! Four! What else can I say? Four!'

The needle must have risen again, but he did not look at it. The heavy, stern face and the four fingers filled his vision. The fingers stood up before his eyes like pillars, enormous, blurry and seeming to vibrate, but unmistakably four.

'How many fingers, Winston?'

'Four! Stop it, stop it! How can you go on? Four! Four!'

'How many fingers, Winston?'

'Five! Five! Five!'

'No, Winston, that is no use. You are lying. You still think there are four. How many fingers, please?'

'Four! Five! Four! Anything you like. Only stop it, stop the pain!'

Abruptly he was sitting up with O'Brien's arm round his shoulders. He had perhaps lost consciousness for a few seconds. The bonds that had held his body down were loosened. He felt very cold, he was shaking uncontrollably, his teeth were chattering, the tears were rolling down his cheeks. For a moment he clung to O'Brien like a baby, curiously comforted by the heavy arm round his shoulders. He had the feeling that O'Brien was his protector, that the pain was something that came from outside, from some other source, and that it was O'Brien who would save him from it.

'You are a slow learner, Winston,' said O'Brien gently.

'How can I help it?' he blubbered. 'How can I help seeing what is in front of my eyes? Two and two are four.'

'Sometimes, Winston. Sometimes they are five. Sometimes they are three. Sometimes they are all of them at once. You must try harder. It is not easy to become sane.'